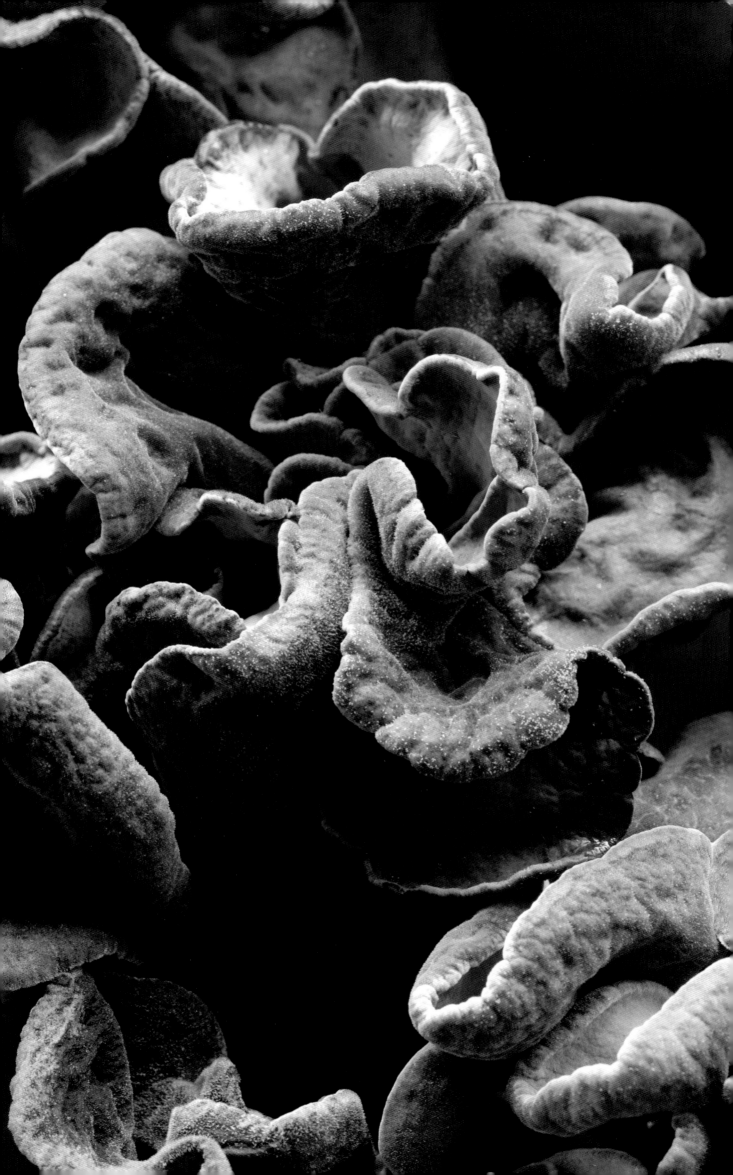

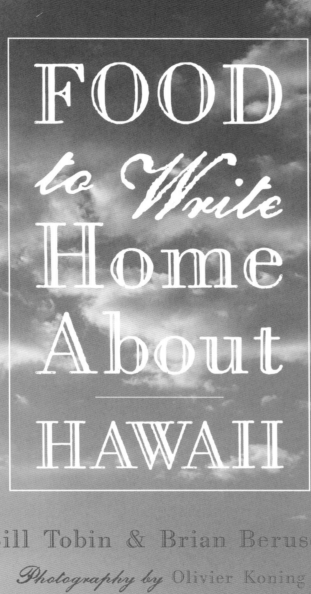

FOOD *to Write* Home About — HAWAII

Bill Tobin & Brian Berusch

Photography by Olivier Koning

CAMERON + COMPANY

Contents

This isn't just a food book.

In these pages, I've detailed my journey from a modest upbringing in the cornfields of Nebraska to the surfer's paradise of Waikiki, where I own a popular restaurant and bar. My journey wasn't extraordinary, but it is a testament to many things: to the determined pursuit of an idea, to following your passion, to making a plan and then getting detoured or derailed, only to find your way to something more grand than you could have dreamed. This is a story about how far you can go by keeping an open mind, by being receptive to misdirection. And exactly how wonderful life can be if you let some new flavors in.

I was born in a small farming community outside of Omaha. Both my grandfathers were farmers: hog, corn and cattle. My father farmed cattle, soybean and corn, too. We ate pork chops with brown gravy and mashed potatoes, all sautéed in a pan. We ate bacon in the mornings that we got from the local "locker"—a polite term for the slaughterhouse that processed our pigs and cattle, packaged the product and stored it until we needed it.

I was happy with all of it. I never had that "I've gotta get out of here!" drive that so many country kids do. I wasn't looking for my golden ticket or filled with teenage angst. Life was good.

There were special moments that leap to mind, a few of which inspired this book. In one, my maternal grandfather, Keith Litel, and I shared a special bond. Grandpa Keith was a big proponent of canned spinach—mind you, this predates the current age—where we tout the provenance of our broccoli stalks. He would heat up the spinach in a pan, and just before serving, dollop a spoonful of vinegar over it. All of my siblings refused. Yet I loved it, and we bonded over that. In the weeks that followed, when he would fry up his own pork chop in the middle of the day, he'd often call me in for a taste. We'd huddle over the stove together, tasting every morsel of the fresh chop in utter silence.

Despite enjoying the quiet Nebraska farm life, I wanted to go to college. So I joined the National Guard to pay for school. With my farm experience I set my sights on a business degree. I was happy with this decision. Yet a far better opportunity would come shortly: the chance to study at the University of Hawaii.

Hawaii! I mean, who—in any of the winter climate zones of the mainland—doesn't dream of spending their Februarys lazing by the beach with a book instead of shoveling driveways? I headed west as quickly as the Army would let me.

Once embedded in university life, I quickly realized that I needed to work to afford to stay in school, let alone have the means to take a girl on a date from time to time. So I got a bar job, then another. And eventually a restaurant gig.

Thus began my true culinary education. Some experiences were palate-opening—like the first time I ate fresh spinach—a giant leap from Grandpa Keith's canned and vinegar coated dish. Others were overwhelming. I had very little exposure to any sort of fish, so my first encounter with a wooden block covered with a rainbow panoply of sashimi was a challenge. Yet these experiences—some that led to lifelong friendships with celebrated chefs—took me on a culinary adventure. There were flavors and ingredients available to me that I never knew existed. They added a dimension to Hawaii living, not yet clear to me then, that set the course for things to come.

Food was my Hawaii gateway drug, as it turns out. Through my passion for the cuisine here, I met and fell in love with my wife. She's of Japanese ancestry, and she further expanded my culinary horizons to include traditions from her Okinawan grandparents. And we are blessed to now have three hapa (half Caucasian, half Asian) sons.

Ultimately my calling took me down the road to opening and owning what's become a celebrated restaurant and bar in Waikiki, just across the street from the world-famous breaks that Duke Kahanamoku surfed nearly a century ago. Tiki's Grill & Bar has become the go-to meeting spot for *pau hana* (after work) drinks and local "grinds" (local slang for food).

Through my dedication to serving top-tier comfort food and by maintaining amicable relationships with fellow restaurateurs across the islands, I'm honored to have been named chairman of the Hawaii Restaurant Association, as well as an officer of other groups like the Young President's Organization, among others.

I can attribute my entire, blessed life here in Hawaii to those early days when my mind was figuratively blown apart and reconstituted by flavors that came to this little archipelago over the past two hundred years. Many are from Japan, China and the Philippines, places from which so many plantation workers migrated in the late nineteenth and early twentieth centuries. Some were brought by visitors from surf cultures in South America and from elsewhere in Polynesia, like Tahiti or Samoa. And some arrived on the Matson ships from the mainland, which also brought swing bands, Babe Ruth, Elvis and the tourism boom that continues today on jet airplanes. Regardless of its origin, the food here has changed my life.

This book is dedicated to my mother, the person to whom I couldn't quite explain what it was about Hawaii that I found so captivating. Yet she was always supportive, always behind me in anything I did. With this book, I'm finally finding the words to tell her this story.

I've approached this book as a series of letters from me to my mother, explaining how a chef, an ingredient or a dining experience changed my perception of food. Reading it, you can follow my evolution. Though I've read it again and again, I still find myself astonished to see the dramatic difference between where I began and where I am now in the world of food.

After each letter to my mom, I introduce the chef who inspired the letter's theme. The chef will then share a recipe that you can replicate in your kitchen. Some are more challenging than others, but all of them are attainable for the savvy home chef. You, too, can plate up a little aloha for your loved ones.

Bear in mind; chefs are very individualistic creatures. Each recipe is presented in measurements that are in keeping with the way they cook. Some have extremely specific directions for their recipes, others (in true Hawaiian style) intentionally leave some ambiguity in order for you to embellish or accommodate ingredients local to your area.

Grab some lilikoi and some pork, some ahi and ginger, some yuzu and some rice, and come along with me on this adventure.

Me ke aloha pumehana,

Bill Tobin

Tiki's Grill & Bar

Mom and I, right after the opening of Tiki's Grill & Bar.

Dear Mom,

I miss you, and I want to share a story about a friend who introduced me to something you'd really enjoy. The story also demonstrates the way economy in food service can benefit what is available at many regional restaurants. It shows how one chef can spotlight an ingredient with such success that it drives the market for that one item—something that might be unique to Hawaii's tightly knit culinary community.

There is a place in my heart—and certainly in my stomach—for Mike Kealoha. Mike worked with us as a line cook at Tiki's for over three years before heading out on his own. And he brought the aloha spirit (while obviously inseparable from his name) to this kitchen, in the design of our menu and food. It's still felt. Mike brims with warmth and gratitude, and his easygoing demeanor belies his mastery.

While working on the line with our chef, Ronnie Nasuti, Mike brought me a dish he insisted I try. He called it "Hawaiian smoke meat" and put it in front of me without saying anything but those three words. He stepped back, crossed his arms, smiled and waited.

Although the description on the menu makes it sound like a stew—protein and veggies piled high on a small bed of rice—this dish is anything but. Whereas a stew is a melding of flavors that have simmered for hours, Mike's dish is cooked hot and fast, with crisp, fresh ingredients, each one a star and competing for attention from your palate.

There were really two elements: the pork itself, cut in 1-inch cubes (I sometimes call it "meat poke" because of the way it's presented), robust and powerful with hints of

sweetness the longer you savored it. Accompanying this were slices of the freshest, locally procured sweet onion, sautéed fast and hot, giving the dish a crunch. Unlike a stew, which might have a gravy poured on top and feel mushy and soft, this was a crisp presentation, both the onions and the meat having dark sear marks on their outsides, yet both bursting with flavor as you bit into them. It was ethereal.

The dish also has a communal appeal. You go at it with a pair of chopsticks, and it's something easily shared at a table. It would be a welcome addition to a tailgate party or a family barbecue. In that way, it's much like ahi poke; put it down and let people pick at the sweet, succulent meat with crisp onions and you'll see a lot of smiles.

Mike's Hawaiian smoke meat not only became a permanent fixture on the Tiki's menu; it's the first thing I order when bringing guests to dine with me. I came to learn two things as I consumed an entire plate of it that day: The first is that the sweetness from the meat came from Hawaiian poha berries. (At least, *some* of the sweetness: Even while working in my kitchen, Mike wouldn't disclose the full list of ingredients. He has since built an entire menu around the item at the successful downtown Honolulu eatery, Highway Inn, where he is the executive chef.)

Poha berries are prized here in the islands. They've appeared in recipes in Hawaii dating as far back as 1830. Likely brought over from Europe in the late eighteenth century on early voyaging ships, they're also called cape gooseberries.

In 2005, when Mike put this dish in front of me, poha berries were not easy to source for a sizable restaurant like ours. You might see them in a roulade painted onto a dish at Chef Mavro's. Or at another small, one-off restaurant where a chef-proprietor has more menu flexibility. But getting consistent delivery of poha berries was not an option at the time.

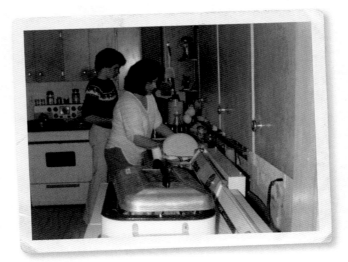

When the dish became popular at Tiki's, Mike made sure to tell to our distributors—and farmers on Oahu, Hawaii Island and Maui— that we needed more poha. Eventually, through what I like to think was the success of this dish at Tiki's (and other restaurants whose chefs would frequent Tiki's after their shifts), other chefs started using poha in more elements on the plate. Soon after, you'd be hard pressed to not find pork ribs glazed with a poha berry BBQ sauce. Or to find poha berries not included in a salad dressing atop some fresh Nalo Greens. And while it's hard to say that one person is responsible for elevating an ingredient, I found it inspirational that Mike's usage ultimately had an effect on what's currently grown and eaten here in Hawaii.

The second thing I learned from Big Mike (the moniker emblazoned on his chef's coat) is that certain foods in Hawaii have a lineage. Mike comes from a family with a long tradition of smoking meat. His siblings, Father and Grandfather all smoke meat in their backyards, garages and kitchens on a regular basis. Whether it's beef, pig, fish or fowl, the Kealohas have logged more hours testing different methods of smoking than possibly anyone serving food here today.

So in tasting his Hawaiian smoke meat at Highway Inn or our version at Tiki's Grill & Bar, guests are literally tasting the experience of generations that have refined a specialty. In Mike's case, it's smoked meat. But it could be a particular presentation of ahi poke, or maybe a banana lumpia dessert. It could be Hawaiian chili water or something else completely. This is very Hawaiian; different families excel at different dishes but all come together to share their best.

I like to think that those with a somewhat refined palate, or at least those who attend to the quality of what they're eating, know authentic Hawaiian fare when they taste it. Anyone can put pineapple on a pizza, but there's no authenticity there. Yet a dish like Mike Kealoha's smoke meat, one that has lineage and history behind it, is inspiring. It's all part of what made me want to learn more, ask questions, delve more deeply, Mom. As my understanding of this place called Hawaii grows, my journey becomes that much more rewarding.

Mom, here is Mike's process for marinating the meats he smokes—you'll love it! Just as Mike's name implies (*kealoha* means "the love"), you can taste his love for Hawaii in each bite.

With love, Bill

Mike Kealoha

"Big Mike" Kealoha is what locals call a "quiet power." Whatever kitchen he's working in, he cooks with passion for everything Hawaiian. He'll always err on the side of staying authentic to the flavors he grew up on, the flavors of old Hawaii. In the local Hawaiian circles, that kind of dedication earns respect. Chefs and restaurateurs all know Mike's face—when he shows up somewhere, the crowds part and he moves to the front. His respect for Hawaii ingredients and preparations has come back to him tenfold.

I hired Mike at Tiki's Grill & Bar during our early days, and he helped transition the kitchen from an assembly line of bar and tourist fare to the sort of dishes I'd come to eat on my days off. The sort of stuff other chefs, bartenders, waiters and anyone else in the food industry would beeline for after their own shifts ended. To me that's a sign of a great chef, one you want on your team.

Mike wears a big smile wherever he goes, so it's no wonder the owners of central Oahu's decades-old favorite, Highway Inn, sought him out when it was time to open a cafe in town. He helped craft a menu so diverse and broad that it can take a bit of time to read through it. This isn't your grandparents' Hawaiian plate lunch diner!

I also love Mike's recipe focusing on smoked meats. There are a lot of great dishes in the pages of this book you can replicate at home. But to have someone lovingly walk you through the steps by which one prepares meat prior to smoking—that's something special. That's a lot of aloha, and I'm sure it will show in the finished product.

Smoke Meat

EARLY HAWAIIANS were known to salt and smoke their meat in order to preserve it for longer in the tropical climate. In modern day Hawaii, many families make a tradition of smoking pork in their backyards, carports or driveways. After the finished product is consumed (with plenty o' cold beer), it's bagged and shared with friends, family and neighbors—it's the Hawaiian way.

Meat

5 pounds, or more, pork butt preferably boneless (easier to cut into steaks)

Hawaiian salt (rock salt)

Marinade

3 cups Shoyu* (soy sauce)

2 cups sugar

1 large finger fresh ginger, minced

5 large cloves fresh garlic, minced

3 pieces Hawaiian chili pepper, minced

*Chef Mike prefers Aloha brand soy sauce. It should be noted that each brand of soy sauce can vary in flavor dramatically. You can experiment with different varieties to see which best suits your palate.

Safety first! Remember to always wash your hands, cutting board and utensils thoroughly after handling pork. And don't cut yourself, just the pork!

Cut the pork butt into "steaks" approximately ¾ to 1 inch thick. There's no rhyme or reason, but don't make them too thin, or the finished pieces could end up dry. Then lay steaks flat and slice into strips. Generously cover the strips with the rock salt.

Combine all the marinade ingredients in a pot on the stove heated to medium. Add the sugar gradually until incorporated well. Cover and refrigerate.

Remove the cooled shoyu-based marinade from the refrigerator and pour it over the pork and toss to coat thoroughly. You can also *lomi* (massage) the marinade into the pork. Cover the pan with foil or plastic wrap (or sealable plastic bag) and place the marinated pork butt into the refrigerator and soak for up to 48 hours. Perhaps you can let it marinate longer, but this is the longest I've done it.

Tools and Fuel of This Trade

Traditionally, many serial smoker enthusiasts have a "smoke house" built specifically for this task. Others may have a commercial or consumer-brand smoker.

My family likes to keep things simple, which I think you'll appreciate: We use a 22-inch Weber Classic charcoal BBQ—the same kind you can find at any hardware store or even many supermarkets.

In Hawaii, we prefer to use *kiawe* (a mesquite varietal) for our smoking wood, as well as some guava tree wood. Any mesquite will do, but I suggest you try a few local varieties to see what creates the flavors you enjoy.

You'll also want at least 5 pounds of charcoal briquettes, which you'll use to start the smoking process. Once they are hot and burning white, add your wood, which has ideally been soaked in water to prevent it from catching fire.

Place the steaks on the grill and cook until done. At Highway Inn we serve it with pan seared sweet onion over white rice . . . but I'm not going to tell you how to eat meat. Find the preparation that works best for you, and make sure you enjoy it with a cold brew.

Serves "Plenty, Brah!"

Dear Mom,

Much like everything in Hawaii, there's a story behind every aspect of our lives here. Do you remember the last time you came out here for Luke's birthday? We had a wonderful cake made for him by a pastry whiz named Abigail Langlas. She's become a friend to our family, having made custom cakes for us on a number of occasions. But the way I met Abi and experienced her mastery of the pastry arts is a tale perfectly suited for this correspondence.

Back when I was opening Tiki's, I put a lot of pressure on myself to deliver. I wanted to prove that we could launch a successful restaurant concept—much easier said than done. The working parts of a restaurant of any size, let alone one the large scope of Tiki's, present so much room for error. I wanted to manage every part of the restaurant so that customers would only rave about the experience.

Just before and right through the opening of Tiki's, I was attending a lot of food events around Honolulu. In the mid-1990s, all these events were stuffy affairs in nondescript

hotel ballrooms, where the banquet chefs would present whatever dishes they could crank out to five hundred people. Then something started happening in the 2000s: Event planners would line the ballrooms with booths manned by leading chefs from around town. They'd prepare and deliver small plates of their favorite dishes or most recent menu items. This fun concept resulted in a more social event where you'd get to try a lot of different foods—and it caught on all over the country, a precursor to the food truck movement.

At a few of these events, I noticed Abi's work. You know I'm not much of a sweets or dessert person, but after trying a dozen dishes from different chefs at one of these events—mostly super-rich, boldly flavored presentations—I was in the mood for a cup of coffee from a local coffee roaster and something sweet.

One of the eye-openers for me was the petit fours from Cafe Laufer, a restaurant and bakery in Kaimuki that has remained under the radar for years. Each dessert was a delightful little package that burst with unique flavors. (I've been picking up samplings of their petit fours for special occasions or gifts ever since.)

At the time we were opening Tiki's, Abi had gone from the pastry chef at Alan Wong's to doing all the food for Honolulu Coffee Company. Through some connections, we (at Tiki's) were asked to make the food for the opening of an upscale shopping center, 2100 Kalakaua Ave.

Because the clientele would be luxury shoppers, we wanted to step up and deliver a delicious single bite. So we opted for a steak dish, hoping that this one bite would put us on the map. In retrospect, it probably wasn't that big a deal, but as the owner of a new restaurant in Waikiki, I was determined to shine. However, I felt that our lead chef at the time wasn't giving me his all for this opportunity. He made a sample for me in the kitchen, which I told him was uninspired. His next attempt wasn't much better.

On the drive home that afternoon, only days before the event, I had an idea. I called Abi and asked her to come in with some ideas. Her first concept was to create a puffed pastry bed on which the steak would rest. It was soft and fluffy but full of buttery flavor that complemented the steak perfectly. Her inspiration truly brought the dish together.

Not only did I gain a new appreciation for the pastry arts and those who focus entirely on desserts, but I was enlightened as to what a collaboration between chefs and restaurateurs can do to elevate a dish. Here I was, stuck with an unexciting dish and a chef who wasn't delivering. Yet by stepping out of the box and bringing in a fresh perspective, we absolutely nailed it. People talked about it for days after, which is precisely what I'd hoped for.

With love, Bill

Abigail Langlas

Abigail Langlas is the chef/owner of Cake Works, a full-scale island bakery specializing in custom cakes. "Chef Abi" makes a variety of breakfast pastries, cookies and special desserts for catering. Most recently, she's produced a full line of colorful, island-inspired French macaroons.

Born in Hilo, Abi's love of the pastry arts led her to Europe. In London, she received a diploma from L'Ecole de Cuisine Francaise de Sabine de Mirbeck and another in advanced pastry from Westminster College. She launched her career with an apprenticeship at London's Four Seasons Hotel, then went to work in Lyon, France, creating desserts for the Restaurant Les Eaux Vives at the four-star Hotel Metropole de Lyon.

Abi moved home to become the in-house pastry chef for Alan Wong, where she created beautiful signature desserts that Wong's team still reveres and that are among the restaurant's most popular menu items. She took a step toward full-time catering when she began creating all the pastries for Honolulu Coffee Company, prior to starting her own bakery.

Abi has made the birthday cakes for my sons as long as they've been alive. It took me a while to realize how special her work is. Every year, depending what the boys are into—sports, movies, books—she will craft a custom cake that relates to their interest. But it's what's on the inside that counts, things like lilikoi or matcha green tea or chai. Abi's opened the door for them to experience flavors I never even dreamed of as an eight-year-old! Yet they scarf them down with vigor—and I couldn't be more proud.

Lilikoi Crunch Cake

LILIKOI (PASSION FRUIT) is a very unique flavor that combines sweet with a touch of sour or tart. But it's universally loved and coveted around the islands. Try and order the purée ahead of time if you cannot find it in your local specialty market, where it should already be available.

Vanilla Chiffon
Preheat the oven to 325°F. Wash two 8-inch round pans in soapy water to make sure they are grease free. Measure the flour, sugar, baking powder, and salt into sifter. Sift into a bowl. Make a well; add the oil, egg yolks, water, and vanilla to the well in the order given. Set aside. Don't beat. In a large mixing bowl, beat the egg whites and cream of tartar until very stiff. Set aside. Using the same beaters, beat the egg yolk batter until smooth and light. Pour gradually over the egg whites, folding in with a rubber spatula. Do not stir. Pour the batter into pans. Bake for 55 minutes. Check if done with a toothpick. Bake for 5 more minutes if not done. Invert the pan on a wire rack until cool. Gently slip a knife around the edge of pan to release the cake, and gently pull from the bottom of the pan to release.

Lilikoi Curd
Crack the eggs into a tall container and use a hand blender to break apart the albumen and yolks into a smooth mixture. Bring the lilikoi purée, sugar and butter to a boil in medium saucepan, stirring to dissolve sugar. Turning down the heat, mix some of the boiling mixture rapidly into the eggs, then quickly transfer back into the saucepan and whisk until the mixture thickens and just begins to simmer. Strain into a container and cool.

Lemon Crunch Candy
Combine the sugar, water, glucose and butter in a large, heavy saucepan. Bring to a boil and continue to boil until the mixture reaches a medium caramel color. Add the lemon extract, then salt and baking soda. Stir until combined, but do not continue to stir as this will deflate the candy. Immediately pour the mixture onto a silicon baking mat or a parchment-lined baking sheet. When completely cool, cut or break apart with something heavy, like the back of your knife. Place immediately into a sealable plastic bag or sealed container until ready to use.

To assemble, reserving ½ cup of the lilikoi curd, take the remaining curd and fold it into the whipping cream. Cut the vanilla chiffons in half horizontally. Spread the first layer of cake with about one-third of the reserved lilikoi curd, then a layer of the lilikoi whip cream mixture; repeat two more times, ending with the last layer of vanilla chiffon. Frost the entire cake with the remaining lilikoi whip cream mixture. Place in the refrigerator for at least 1 hour. When ready to present, take the lemon candy and crush into small pieces. Cover the entire cake with candy. Do not do this more than 2 hours ahead of time, or the candy will start to melt.

Serves 4

Vanilla Chiffon
- 2 cups sifted cake flour
- 1½ cups white sugar
- 1 tablespoon baking powder
- 1 teaspoon salt
- ½ cup vegetable oil
- 7 egg yolks
- ¾ cup cold water
- 2 teaspoons vanilla extract
- 7 egg whites
- ½ teaspoon cream of tartar

Lilikoi Curd
- 10 eggs
- 1 cup lilikoi purée
- 1½ cups sugar
- 1½ cups butter

Lemon Crunch Candy
- 2 cups sugar
- ¼ cup water
- ¼ cup corn syrup
- ¼ cup butter
- 1 teaspoon lemon extract
- ¼ teaspoon salt
- 1 teaspoon baking soda, sifted

- 2 cups Lilikoi Curd
- 4 cups whipped heavy cream, no sugar added
- 2 eight-inch vanilla chiffons
- 1 recipe lemon candy

Aloha Mom,

Today was a day I think you truly would have appreciated. Growing up, you, Dad and Grandpa made sure we always had fresh farmed dairy goods. Needless to say, eggs were never in short supply—they were the "building block" of farm life, really. And, like families on or off farms across America, we ate our share: omelettes, over easy, hard boiled, egg salad, deviled eggs. Although they came in many styles, they never ventured too far from their original state. I remember seeing an egg being dropped into a large bowl when you were making cookies, or a birthday cake, somehow disappearing into the sugary goodness. I guess I always knew they had a bigger role than a breakfast food, but until today, I never really considered what that could be.

Jon Matsubara is one of the quieter, softer spoken chefs in Honolulu. He doesn't promote himself like a lot of the others, or cook at large events much. But he has impeccable training, is very well-spoken, and frankly, just completely shocked all my preconceived notions of what an egg can do as the "main attraction" on a plate.

In case you don't already know, Mom, molecular gastronomy is using science-like techniques to change the perception and/or presentation of an ingredient. Jon Matsubara

was the first person to plate for me dishes that made use of the practice, which I'd only seen on competitive television shows. I had thought it was a flashy, show-off way to tweak food that usually fell short on flavor. But Jon really changed my mind with the most simplest items of all—the egg.

I'll do my best to describe it to you, Mom, but remember, I'm not a chef. In short, Chef Jon removes the egg from the shell, blends it with some incredible ingredients, scrambles it over heat, whisking the entire time it cooks to whip air into the egg molecules, and then he returns the mixture into the egg shell. It's presented at the table with a tiny spoon, and you take tiny, delicate bites that explode with flavor in your mouth.

When I think about the many childhood days of sopping up the sticky, runny yolk with a piece of white toast . . . it's a far cry, Mom, from the delicate spoonfuls I lifted to my mouth as if I were eating caviar. It was so far out of my comfort zone, but I realized something during and after the experience: when you're presented with something you "know"—in this case, an egg—and then what's inside is nothing that resembles the properties you've assigned to that item, it takes a certain open-mindedness or change in the brain to accept that it could be something good. I think the average human wants to say "Oh no, that's not how I like *my* eggs," but it's about something more than that. It's about experiencing something you're not expecting—and being open to new ideas.

If you can muster the gall to accept this new presentation, you'll be the better for it. A door is opened: the world expands from oysters to oyster sauce. Everything that once was—can now be something completely new. It simply takes the innovation of a talented chef, like Jon, to open your eyes to the possibilities.

There's a life lesson in there somewhere, Mom! I'm sure you'd have come up with it in perfect wording.

With love, Bill

Jon Matsubara

Jon Matsubara has reinvented himself as the "it" chef of Honolulu several times. Yet he's far from a "go where the wind blows" chef; he's steeped in great experience, having trained with some of the best chefs in Hawaii as well as world-renown talent on the mainland.

Born and raised in Honolulu, Jon's "a-ha" moment came in an unlikely place—a law school classroom in San Diego. While listening to a fellow student answer questions about case law, Jon had an epiphany: He could never be passionate about law. He walked out of the class and called Russell Siu, owner of the popular 3660 on the Rise restaurant in Kaimuki, Oahu, who connected him with a restaurant job at Four Seasons in San Diego. After a short stint, the luster wore off California life, so he packed up and returned home.

He approached both Alan Wong and Roy Yamaguchi, but neither was hiring. So he made a deal: He would wash dishes and come in four hours early to learn sauces, assisting wherever help was needed. He learned every station during that unorthodox three-year apprenticeship.

Next he jumped to New York City, completing a training at the French Culinary Institute, where, as he recalls, "I met all-star New York chefs who liked me because instead of learning basic knife cuts, I wanted to know about braising." This earned him a spot in a David Bouley kitchen, followed by Tabla, a Danny Meyer restaurant. Feeling as though he could handle one more upscale eatery, Meyer's chef Floyd Cardoz got him into Jean-Georges, where Jon worked as *chef de partie* for two years, manning the fish station and perfecting his sauces.

What I appreciate about Jon's story is that through all of this, his wife was by his side. She was in law school in New York and was able to practice there, as with each move they made—California, Hawaii, New York. The pair have grown together on this worldwide food journey, something that strikes a chord with me.

When it was time to head home to Hawaii, Jon talked to the chef at Mauna Lani Resort on Hawaii Island, who offered him a rare open spot. Although it was manning the hotel's breakfast service, Jon isn't one to miss an opportunity. He initiated a breakfast tasting menu at a time when most hotel restaurants were churning out big metal trays of scrambled eggs and kalua pork hash. This quickly moved him up the ranks to Canoe House at Mauna Lani, a great bump—or so it would seem.

"I didn't move back to Hawaii to do Hawaii Regional Cuisine and had reservations in taking the role," says Jon. "Alan Wong talked me into it, and the move turned out to be a good one." It was during his stint there that Honolulu real estate developer Thomas Sorensen asked him to open Stage restaurant at the Honolulu Design Center, where he could design his own kitchen, no budget limits.

He brought the eatery up to cult status before jumping to Azure at the Royal Hawaiian, a recently renovated, sexy eatery that allowed him to stretch his wings with a food-savvy clientele from all corners of the globe. I remember an epic dish he executed there, in which the waiter removed a glass bell from over the plate and a cloud of fragrant *kiawe* (mesquite) woodsmoke wafted across the table.

Jon took over Japengo at the Hyatt Regency in Waikiki before settling at Forty Carrots, the restaurant inside the new Bloomingdales at Ala Moana Center. Clearly the international, well-traveled set is his ideal clientele. And you can expect to see him exquisitely plating nouveau American, Japanese, European and molecular gastronomy styles wherever he lands.

Tamago Caviar

"I LEARNED this dish from Jean-Georges Vongerichten in New York City. He used to make a similar version for VIPs every night. I worked directly next to him, observing as he whisked the eggs forever to get a creamy, luxurious texture. He used to serve it with vodka whipped cream and beluga caviar—something he confided he learned from his mentor, Chef Paul Bucose. At Stage and Azure restaurants, I used Italian black truffles; at Japengo we did it with an Asian twist on dashi tamago and marinated ikura."

To make the bacon dashi, bring the konbu to a boil and simmer for 1 hour. Remove from the heat and add the bonito flakes and the bacon. Let steep for 30 minutes, strain and set the liquid (dashi) aside.

In a small pot, add the butter, cream, eggs, and ½ cup bacon dashi and whisk for 12 minutes on medium-low heat. Season with salt and pepper. When the egg begins to coagulate into a runny "pancake" viscosity, remove from the heat and add the chives. Spoon into egg shells until three-quarters full and top with the croutons and a generous mound of ikura. Garnish with the chervil sprig.

Serves 4

Bacon Dashi

2 (6-inch) pieces konbu

2 tablespoons toasted bonito flakes

½ pound smoky bacon

2½ tablespoons butter

½ cup cream

4 eggs

Salt and pepper

4 egg shells with top removed

1 tablespoon chopped chives

¼ cup small-diced sourdough croutons

4 tablespoons ikura marinated in sake, mirin and salt water

4 chervil sprigs, for garnish

Dear Mom,

As a family, we visit Tango Contemporary Cafe downtown for breakfast or brunch at least twice per month. I almost always order Chef Goran Streng's homemade bircher muesli. I've said before, I don't have much of a sweet tooth, but this is really, really good—yet I somehow feel healthy after eating it.

Growing up on the farm in Nebraska, I loved it when Grandmother (your mom) made me oatmeal. I remember staying over at her and Grandpa's house—something I really grew to appreciate, now—that bond I was able to forge with them. They were

classic American farmers; I can still recall Grandfather's bib overalls and flannel shirt, which he wore every day. We all remember, too, what a penny pincher he was! (After his passing we found ledgers that detailed every nickel spent for decades. He had notes on where my uncles, his sons, spent money on sticks of gum in high school!)

He worked hard and led a good life.

Anyway, Mom: The way Grandmother would cook the oatmeal low and slow over a stove—this was the pre-instant era after all—slowly adding sugar, butter and milk, stirring while she watched us scamper out of bed to watch the process. I may have not known it then, but this ritual became a part of the allure of the dish. We were forming memories attached to food, and it has stuck with me to this day, almost a half century later.

In the evenings, it was Grandpa's turn. He was a big spinach fan. Back then, it was funny (and somewhat unfortunately) to think that "exotic" came in the form of canned spinach. As mentioned elsewhere in this book, I still find it funny that most people think farmers grow up surrounded by fresh veggies all the time. But this was the 1960s and '70s. Flash freezing and canning were the technology of the day, and so that's how most things came. And second, as a farming family, we pinched every dime we could and lived accordingly.

None of my siblings would touch the stuff. But Grandpa had this way . . . he'd serve it with a tablespoon of vinegar over it, and I loved it. The way the flavor of the spinach changed so dramatically with this simple addition just shocked my taste buds, and it became this bond between us. So more and more he'd make it, and more and more I'd relish in this act, our special bond.

Once in a while, he'd come home with a pork chop and fry it up himself in a cast iron pan. He'd call me into the kitchen—everyone assuming it was to share some canned spinach—and we'd fork down on a meaty chop in near silence. Even though Grandma ran the kitchen, he took the helm for his occasional chop. And it became another ritual that I have deep memories of.

Eating at Tango, a lot of these memories come rushing to the front of my mind. Maybe it's the fairly barren, clean decor of the cafe. Perhaps it's the simplicity of the food, yet dedication to spotlighting the best of each component of the plate. This is very Scandinavian and apropos of Chef Streng. But for me, it's a great opportunity.

Over my bircher muesli, I share the stories of my grandmother and grandfather with my three boys, who couldn't have more different upbringings than I did. From the beaches of Oahu to the farms of Nebraska is a big leap. I can close the gap by sharing these stories over great food. And I feel fortunate they will listen!

Whatever it is, it's working. My son Luke orders the spinach salad there, every time. Tracy and I are always amazed—neither of us could imagine ordering a spinach salad (voluntarily!) when we were his age. And yet, it's not hard to see why. The greens are firm and crisp. Chef Streng's unique preparation features thinly sliced scallops, which he sears in a tangy brown butter sauce that's finished with a pomegranate vinaigrette. Watching my son hunt for the scallops, fork them over a few leaves of spinach, and find bits of onion to pair and then devour at a rapid pace . . . I feel so lucky for so many reasons. But selfishly, it's a direct tie to my grandparents, who he never got to meet. By sharing those stories over this dish, it's passing on tradition. One leaf at a time.

With love, Bill

Goran V. Streng

In this tropical, far-flung destination, chef Goran V. Streng might have the most foreign background. Co-owner and chef of the wonderful Tango Contemporary Cafe in Honolulu's Kakaako-Ward area, Streng hails from Finland.

He is a Helsinki Hotel and Restaurant School graduate, has traveled with the Finnish Navy, and cooked for ambassadors in Yugoslavia prior to "discovering" Hawaii and the allure of its culinary wonders.

Streng dug into the structured hotel circuit, working at La Mer in the Halekulani, on Hawaii (Big) Island at the Ritz Carlton (now the Fairmont Orchid) and Mauna Kea Beach Hotel. He did a stint on Maui at the old Kapalua Bay Hotel and jumped to one of the world's most spectacular venues—Raffles Hotel in Singapore.

While the warm water fish are night and day from the frigid Scandinavian waters and the cuisine there, Streng has found great passion in utilizing the availability of product here. His manner of melding the healthy grains and preparations of Scandinavian foods with Hawaii's bounty has proven successful with residents and visitors, as Streng has a quiet army of dedicated followers. So much so, that he's represented the islands in various marketing campaigns and efforts, such as cooking for top national media at New York's James Beard House.

Tango Contemporary Cafe, tucked into a quiet location off Queen Street in the revitalized Kakaako area at the base of the Hokua Building, serves breakfast, brunch, lunch and dinner. The space is awash in clean white, ultramodern lighting fixtures and colorful art. There's a clean aesthetic to the architecture and surrounding space that lends to Streng's background and suits his cuisine. It's a fresh change for Hawaii.

Streng frequently features cold-water fish, and sometimes he'll serve them smoked. One aspect that's always a treat—and not typically common knowledge—is that he crafts most of his own condiments at Tango. He told me once that it was to challenge himself to create everything he puts on the plate. But knowing the chef's mind, I believe he just has to figure out how he can elevate his ketchup, mayonnaise and aioli to suit the dishes they accompany. Just another reason to pass through the Tango doors for a meal.

Smoked Duck Breast and Duck Leg Confit, Sweet Kahuku Corn Polenta, Poha Berry Demi-Glace

THIS HEARTY DISH combines wintry elements like duck breast, confit and polenta with the powerful demi-glace made from Hawaiian poha berries. You can replace the berries at your preference, opting for something more easily accessible but still with a strong flavor profile. Cranberries, plums, peaches or diced up nectarines would be the chef's top choices.

Preheat the oven to 250°F.

Duck Leg Confit

Place the duck legs in a medium-size pan, sprinkle with half of the salt, rub it in thoroughly, cover and refrigerate overnight. The next day, rinse off the salt and place the legs in a heavy ovenproof dish, sprinkle with the rest of the salt, add the garlic, thyme, bay leaves and pepper. Cover with duck fat or oil. Bake in the preheated oven for 8 hours. Alternatively, cook on the stove top in a heavy cast iron crock pot on very low heat, at a light simmer, until the meat falls off the bone, about 5 hours. When done, let it cool in the fat. Once cooled, remove the duck legs and separate the fat from the duck jus at the bottom, to be used for the sauce.

Smoked Duck Breast

Score the skin of the duck breast, and season with salt and pepper on both sides. Place on a rack in a smoker on low heat for 45 minutes, or until about medium rare.

Creamy Polenta

In a small pot over medium, melt the butter and sauté the shallots. Add the thyme, chicken broth and corn kernels. Using a wooden spoon slowly pour in corn meal, and simmer until creamy, about 3–5 minutes.

Poha Berry Demi-Glace

Place the balsamic vinegar in a small sauté pan over high heat and reduce until almost dry. Add the poha berries and duck jus, reduce by half, about 2 minutes.

To plate, quickly sauté the carrots, broccoli and peas on the stovetop, set aside. In a large, heavy skillet over high heat, sauté the duck breast and legs with skin side down until crisp. Place the creamy polenta on a plate, then lean the duck leg on the polenta. Slice the duck breast and arrange in front of the leg. Place the sautéed vegetables around, and top with the poha berry demi-glace. Garnish with the pea tendrils.

Serves 4

Duck Leg Confit

4 duck legs

½ cup kosher salt

¼ cup peeled garlic cloves

6 sprigs fresh thyme

3 bay leaves

1 tablespoon whole black pepper

2 cups duck fat or vegetable oil

Smoked Duck Breast

4 duck breast, smoked

Salt and pepper

Creamy Polenta

1 tablespoon butter

1 tablespoon shallots, chopped

2 sprigs thyme leaves

2 cups chicken broth

¼ cup roasted corn kernels

¾ cup corn meal

Poha Berry Demi-Glace

2 tablespoons balsamic vinegar

⅓ cup poha berries

1 cup duck jus

Baby carrots

Romanesco broccoli

Sugar snap peas

Sugar snap pea tendrils, for garnish

Dear Mom,

I'm pretty excited to tell you about this next chef because I truly believe we have yet to see his full potential realized on the dining scene in Hawaii. I'm not alone in thinking so. Chris Kajioka is young, and nearly every foodie in Hawaii (or San Francisco or New York) agrees he's a rising star. At the time of this writing, we've only begun to see the first bursts from this talent. I genuinely believe he could be our next Chef Mavro.

Chris has earned a reputation that follows on the heels of his impeccable training. He graduated from the Culinary Institute of America in Hyde Park and worked in Thomas Keller's Per Se. Most people here first heard his name when he was hand-picked by an eccentric Japanese businessman to open Vintage Cave, an experiment of a restaurant where twenty courses were the norm and ingredients shipped in from every corner of the world. Chris wowed many during his stint there, satisfying the palates of those who could afford the heart-stopping bill and were eager to taste Chris's inventive take on trends occurring in kitchens outside Hawaii. He was the right man to deliver.

As strange as it sounds, Chris's process reminds me of something from my own childhood. I have fond memories of waking before dawn to bring hay to the cattle with Dad. After we'd stacked the golden bales, we'd hunt for freshly sprouted morel mushrooms, filling a paper lunch sack with the fungi before heading home. I remember the first time we plucked them out of the ground, thinking, "What are we going to do with these weird things?" Eating them was the furthest thing from my mind.

We brushed off the dirt, washed them in egg whites, dusted them with flour and covered them with crumbled Saltines. Then we baked them. During the process, I wasn't sure I wanted to take a bite. But then the golden, earthy caps came off the stove and filled the kitchen with a unique scent. And they were delicious! I was transformed, as was my belief that something seemingly foul (fungus growing in the dirt) couldn't be delicious. Kajioka's cooking taps into this same contradiction. Every dish of his I've tasted turns something in it on its head in the most wonderful way.

Chris is a stereotypical chef in the sense that he lets his food speak for him, but his public statements only amplify the excitement of foodies in this town. He's spoken of his disdain for the pigeon-hole of Hawaii Regional Cuisine, the movement that put these islands on the global food map in the late 1980s. Hawaii's been "stuck" doing merely Asian fusion ever since, he says. Chris believes that our plethora of amazing ingredients, our fish and ranched produce, could be showcased in more original presentations, and he's thus far showed us he's the right man to do it.

What's perhaps most astounding about Chris is that wherever he's cooked, he's had his pick of the finest ingredients from all over the world. And yet he's championed many homegrown Hawaii products; he genuinely believes they are world-class. Here's a young chef reflecting some of his well-deserved celebrity spotlight and casting it onto ingredients produced on a small chain of islands in the mid-Pacific—and including them in previously unseen dishes. Edible flowers, micro greens and even strawberries from upcountry Maui are just a few examples.

It's been said that some of Chris's dishes make more conservative diners uncomfortable because he's turning traditional dishes on their heads. I have found this to be true, yet Chris somehow manages to always—*always*—preserve the integrity of flavors and essence of a dish. Like chefs Mavro and Vasquez (who come first to mind), Chris can take familiar, local ingredients and prepare them in a unique way—a mind-blowing presentation or the addition of one flavor that completely alters the way you perceive the dish.

An example of this is one of his fish preparations I tasted in which he included an unlikely garnish: popcorn. On the crisped skin side of the fish, he'd added a caramelized sauce. To complement it, Chris finished the dish with crisp, caramelized popcorn. This did two things for me: First, it utterly surprised me. Who expects popcorn at a high-end restaurant? On a fish dish? Shocking, it was a great textural and visceral element. It wasn't just a gimmick; it truly added to the flavor components.

Second, it had a personal connection for me—something Chris couldn't have known, but as I mentioned earlier, a good chef knows how to connect to a diner's emotions. Mom, you probably remember the summers when I was 11 or 12 years old, when Dad sold popcorn. Together we'd make the hour drive to the Jiffy Pop corn elevator. We'd drive down with our haul—what seemed like a massive amount of popcorn kernels to me—until we saw other farmers arriving with wagons and semitrucks, pouring tons of kernels into the elevator.

We'd harvest so much that we'd be searching for every tin, bottle, can and even our wooden wagons to store popcorn in. You'll probably remember, Mom, at Christmas that year you packaged a number of bottles that we gave as gifts.

That piece of popcorn connects me to my boys as well. Every year they sell a variety of flavored popcorn as a fundraiser for their Cub Scout Pack. I take them to Waikiki, and we walk around selling—but not before insisting they listen to me talk about driving with my dad to the Jiffy elevator! A little different from the days of hauling sacks of kernels with Dad, but a connection nonetheless. And to think, you can walk into Neiman Marcus and there are $60 tins of popcorn!

The community of Honolulu chefs and adventurous diners are all excited to try Senia, Chris's new restaurant in Chinatown. We're anticipating the culinary surprises he'll put before us. Thanks for reading, Mom.

With love, Bill

Chris Kajioka

hris Kajioka received his formal training from the Culinary Institute of America in New York's Hudson Valley. He went on to work at Ron Siegel's Dining Room at the Ritz-Carlton in San Francisco, followed by Thomas Keller's Per Se in New York. After logging some more West Coast time at Aziza and Willow Inn in Washington State, Hawaii called. Chris was lured home with a unique offer: To be the opening executive chef at a wild experiment called Vintage Cave, an underground vanity project for a wealthy Japanese supermarket scion who wished to create a club-like atmosphere. With virtually no limits on ingredients—Chris could spend whatever he wanted and source from anywhere he wished on the globe—it was a dream gig for a chef ready to spread his wings.

A typical tasting menu at Vintage Cave featured up to twenty courses, with wine pairings that ran the gamut. Word of his inventive style spread quickly through the upper echelons of Oahu society, eventually luring foodies from neighbor islands and adventuresome visiting culinarians. Before his stint wrapped, he had earned a nomination for James Beard's Rising Star Award and concocted a dish that was listed on *Food & Wine* magazine's "Top 10 Dishes of 2013."

Thanks to his James Beard nod, Chris earned a scholarship to travel the world and taste his way around. Upon returning, he added the title of new dad to his resume before packing up the family and heading back to the Bay Area to help friend (and former Aziza chef) Mourad Lahlou open his signature eatery as chef de cuisine. The lively San Francisco culinary and mixology scene inspired Chris, who was all the while distilling a concept for his own restaurant back home. He returned and secured a space in Chinatown directly next door to the Pig and the Lady, a popular restaurant run by his friend, respected chef Andrew Le.

As of this writing, Chris's new restaurant, Senia, will open in Spring 2016.

He's partnered with another former coworker, Anthony Rush, whom he met at Per Se. Rush, who most recently helmed Fera in London's Claridge's Hotel, brings his wife Katherine to the mix, who will manage the front of the house at Senia.

"The word *senia* is Greek for 'hospitality.' We're going to try and have a lot of fun here," Chris says. He plans to employ many former culinary students from around Hawaii, as he's eager to elevate local emerging talent.

At all of thirty-two years of age, the future certainly seems bright for Chris Kajioka.

Poached Aromatic Chicken with Chive-Garlic Sauce

CHRIS HAS MADE a name for himself with his highly technical preparations. He can utilize a wide array of ingredients on each plate, yet every element will find a place and a reason for involvement within the dish. So we consider it a blessing that Chris was eager to share one of his simpler, more easily prepared dishes that delivers high-value for minimal effort. And of course, following the more simplistic direction of a highly meticulous chef will only "up" your chops when it comes to the fancy stuff . . . down the road. What makes this dish is the aromatic usage of fresh herbs, as both a sauce and in the preparation of the chicken.

Prepping the "Aromatics"

In a small pot over medium heat, brown the ginger, garlic, sugar and shallots using the canola oil. Once lightly browned, add in the soy, vinegar, fish sauce and sesame oil. Simmer everything together for 2 minutes without reducing, then remove from the heat and add the chives.

Chicken Breast

Poach the chicken breasts in a small pot with cold water to cover, adding the ginger, garlic and chives. Also add in 1 teaspoon of kosher salt per breast to the water. Bring the cold water, aromatics and chicken breast up to a simmer. Simmer for 3 minutes and shut off the heat. Let sit in hot broth for 20 minutes or until cool.

When serving, slice room temperature chicken breast. Heat the sauce and ladle to cover.

Serves 4 to 6

Chive Garlic Sauce

3 tablespoons ginger, minced

2 tablespoons garlic, minced

¼ cup sugar

3 tablespoons shallots, thinly sliced

4 tablespoons canola oil

4 ounces dark soy

3 tablespoons Chinese black vinegar

1 tablespoon fish sauce

1 teaspoon sesame oil

4 tablespoons tubular chives, thinly sliced

4 chicken breasts

1 teaspoon ginger

1 teaspoon garlic

1 teaspoon chives

1 teaspoon kosher salt per breast in water

Dear Mom,

Do you remember when I graduated from the University of Hawaii back in 1995? I had a fresh business degree and headed into the construction industry. Pushing papers around a desk isn't the worst way to earn a check. But during the two years I spent in construction, I couldn't help but reminisce about the years I'd worked in bars and restaurants to help pay for college. There was something about the camaraderie and the reward of serving people good food and drink that made the employees—and me—very happy. It's your job to deliver someone a fun experience. My path was becoming clearer.

What you might not know is that when I finally made the leap back into hospitality, it was as manager at the Hard Rock Cafe. I had the honor of working for Rob Goldberg, who went on to become a senior vice-president for Tommy Bahama, a great company that's expanded from clothing and lifestyle garments to restaurants and bars. (Rob was also president of PlumpJack Wine Group for a stint.)

As you know, I'd never worked a job that came with an expense account, so this was the first time I had a little money in my pocket—which meant I could justify spending some of it on a nice meal if I wanted to take a girl out to dinner. When that occasion arose, I asked Rob where I should go. "Alan Wong's," he said, without skipping a beat.

Alan's South King Street signature restaurant was relatively new. I made a reservation unsure of what to expect and showed up with the girl I was dating. The somewhat odd entry (you take an elevator up three floors from a parking garage to the restaurant) only heightened the feeling that we were being physically transported, not yet knowing that our palates would be figuratively transported, too.

We were escorted onto the lanai, which overlooks the Koolau mountains, distant lights twinkling from the homes on the ridge. From the moment we sat until the moment we left, the staff provided a level of service I had yet to experience. The hostess gracefully

handing us menus; a busser delivering bread and water; the waitress immediately taking our drinks order and talking us through the menu . . . it went on and on. The attention to detail and the refined nature of the dishes were the difference between "going out to dinner" and "having a dining experience."

Our other big impression involved the food itself. I know you're well aware that we didn't eat a lot of fish growing up in Nebraska. Unless you wanted frozen fish sticks, seafood just wasn't an option. I made the jump to eating fish in my twenties, occasionally ordering salmon if it was from the Pacific Northwest. Although I considered it a "fishy" fish (salmon is oily), at the time I just assumed that all fish had similar properties. My experience at Alan Wong's changed all that.

Being so well served for the first time—and on a date, no less—I ordered outside my comfort zone. The chef featured a local fish called opakapaka, a pink snapper with delicate, white meat. Mochi, a glutinous rice pounded into a paste and sometimes sweetened, was wrapped around the fish. Underneath was a local Hamakua mushroom risotto and a buttery, tangy sauce beneath that.

The slightly sweet mochi gave way to a succulent fish that was light and airy yet still slightly oily. It was by no means as rich as the salmon I knew, and it took some time to recognize that the fish before me was even the same species. It was otherworldly. Piercing the mochi to take a forkful of tender white fish, a bit of risotto and finishing the bite with the sauce . . . each mouthful was transportive. Talk about setting the mood on a date! That seductive plate commanded my full attention—I probably gave it more than I gave to my date. My mind was blown.

We finished the meal with stunning desserts and his hand-selected French press coffee that Alan sources from Kau, a lesser-known growing region on Hawaii Island. I didn't want to leave.

Mom, I have the feeling I will look back at certain pivotal moments throughout my time here in Hawaii—in my career, relationships and so forth. But in the food dimension of my life, that first eloquent meal at Alan Wong's lit a fire inside me. I will be eating more of this food. More importantly, I will be taking steps to work harder solely so I can afford to eat like this more regularly. It's a must.

With love, Bill

Alan Wong

Y ou cannot begin a conversation about the talent that has spun out of Hawaii Regional Cuisine without speaking of Alan Wong. Alan combines his multicultural background with schooling in the French culinary arts. He worked on the line at Lutece in New York City, when Lutece was *the* place for the jet-set and glitterati of the 1980s. There he gleaned a lifetime's worth of aphorisms from Chef Andre Soltner—which Alan would later carry with him back to Hawaii and launch an empire.

Alan's island journey started in 1989 at the Canoe House in the Mauna Lani Bay Hotel on Hawaii Island. It was there that he began forging what would become lifelong relationships with local farmers, ranchers, coffee growers and fishermen. Alan was among the group of eleven other Hawaii chefs who birthed Hawaii Regional Cuisine—at the time, a revolution in food standards in Hawaii. Hawaii Regional Cuisine called on the cultural aspects of food rather than rely on frozen, cookie-cutter imitations of what people think of as "tropical island fare." The movement sent shockwaves through the culinary world and set the table for the global phenomenon that is Asian fusion cuisine.

In 1994 organizations like Robert Mondavi, *Sante Magazine*, James Beard and *Bon Appétit* started looking to Alan as a leader in Hawaii's culinary renaissance. In 1995 he opened Alan Wong's on King Street, and the following year he received the Beard nomination for Best New Restaurant while taking home the Beard award for Best Chef Pacific Northwest.

Alan went on to open the Pineapple Room inside Macy's at Ala Moana Center in 1999. He's published various cookbooks and opened eateries on neighbor islands, including Hualalai Grille on Hawaii Island. The youngest member of Alan's empire is Alan Wong's Shanghai, in China.

Perhaps most significantly, more top chef talent earned their stripes in Alan's kitchens than anywhere else in the islands. He's a mentor of the highest order and a champion of the farmers, ranchers and fishermen throughout the state who provide top ingredients to Hawaii. Alan periodically dedicates an evening at Alan Wong's to the product of a single farmer—his Farmer's Series Dinners—which sells out in advance and has a rabid following.

Alan works closely with the culinary school at Kapiolani Community College (now called the Culinary Institute of the Pacific) to share his wisdom and experience with emerging local talent. As intimidating as he can seem in person, Alan is a generous soul who perpetually aims to shine the best possible light on Hawaii cuisine. Finally, it's no wonder that President Barack Obama makes a point to eat at Alan Wong's every December when he visits his island home.

Caesar Salad

SELECTING A **Caesar** salad is uniquely emblematic of the Alan Wong experience, and why it's perfect for inclusion in this book. While dining at one of Wong's restaurant is a melange of flavors, colors and presentation, nearly everything he does comes back to sourcing the absolute best produce he can find. And when you consider his longevity and accomplishments in the Hawaii food scene, you know that what he is sourcing is the best. Here, each leaf of lettuce, tomato, and dressing component are meticulously honed by various chefs on the Wong team. It isn't uncommon to hear a diner departing Alan Wong's say: "I've had a lot of salads, but none like that!"

Alan serves this with his slow-roasted Kalua Pig, but you can add your favorite protein.

Anchovy Dressing

In a blender, combine the egg, yolk, anchovies, garlic, vinegar, Worcestershire sauce, mustard, lemon juice, and water. With the machine running, slowly add the oil until it is completely incorporated. Season with salt. Refrigerate until needed.

Crispy Cheese Baskets

To prepare the cheese baskets, sprinkle 1 cup of the cheese evenly in a 6-inch nonstick pan. Place over low heat for about 2 minutes, or until the cheese melts together into a sheet and begins to bubble. While still warm and pliable, drape the sheet over the end of an upturned tumbler or soda can. Mold the cheese so that it forms a basket; as it cools it will harden and keep its basket shape. Remove from the glass or can and invert. Repeat for the remaining 3 baskets.

To serve, drizzle 1 tablespoon of the Anchovy Dressing around each of the individual plates. Place a cheese basket in the middle of each plate and stand 6 lettuce leaves upright inside each basket. Fill the baskets with the cut lettuce. Drizzle 1 tablespoon of the Anchovy Dressing over the lettuce in each basket. Top with an anchovy fillet and 1 teaspoon of the grated cheese. Top with the croutons scattered around. Accompany with the remaining Anchovy Dressing and protein of your choice.

Serves 4

Anchovy Dressing

1 egg, plus 1 yolk

5 anchovy fillets

1 teaspoon minced garlic

1 tablespoon red wine vinegar

1 teaspoon Worcestershire sauce

1 teaspoon Dijon mustard

½ tablespoon freshly squeezed lemon juice

½ cup water

1 cup olive oil

Salt to taste

Crispy Cheese Baskets

4 cups grated Parmesan cheese

24 whole baby romaine lettuce leaves, plus 4–6 small romaine heads cut into 1-inch segments

4 anchovy fillets

4 teaspoons finely grated Parmesan cheese

1 cup toasted croutons

Alan shared with us an interesting aspect to his menu planning: As dishes graduate to being considered for inclusion on his menu, he will photograph a finalized plate himself, from multiple angles. He'll then retreat to his office and look at the images on a computer, which allows him to see it from a unique perspective. "Is the dish missing an element? A color splash? Is it balanced? These are all things I might see in the image that I might not get from physically holding the dish," Wong shares.

Dear Mom,

I recently had the opportunity to walk through three restaurants owned by Mark Ellman, one of the founders of Hawaii Regional Cuisine. Mark is an interesting personality here in Hawaii; he's a Los Angeles–raised chef who moved to the islands in the mid-1980s and immediately earned a following through a Maui restaurant he opened called Avalon.

He went on to launch an island-inspired taco trend (Maui Tacos, which he sold in 2008) and has a penchant for partnering with high-profile investors in the entertainment industry. He recently opened a Mexican-themed restaurant called Frida's (as in Frida Kahlo). This chef-restaurateur with the Midas touch managed to secure a stunning location on Front Street in Lahaina—a bustling, historic whaling village that's the tourism hub of West Maui. Mark's three thriving restaurants, Frida's, Mala and Honu, are all adjacent in a row, tucked between the road and the ocean, with the best tables at each on a lanai over the water. As

diners dig into their incredibly fresh fish, they can watch huge sea turtles nibbling on *limu* (seaweed) in the afternoon sun.

The decor at each restaurant varies slightly, but to me there's something that harks back to the old seafood shacks of New England: the low ceilings, the sound of seabirds outside and the ridiculously fresh fish—expertly cut within hours of coming in from the fish auction.

Remember the single-take scene in *Goodfellas* where Ray Liotta's character walks from the parking lot in through the kitchen and to the front of the restaurant, where an impromptu table is set just for him? That's how I felt as Mark walked me through Frida's, then Honu, then into a walk-in freezer (where I saw the most magnificent yellowfin tuna) and into a seat at Mala for a chat. When I think about his three different concepts at three locations, each kitchen within shouting distance of the next . . . it's pretty amazing.

It's easy to see how Mark became a key figure in Hawaii Regional Cuisine: He's super genuine, gracious and a natural leader. But he's also a master of highlighting Hawaii's fresh, unique flavor profiles and then melding them into approachable dishes that on the surface seem familiar to the diner. There's a distinct comfort to his food, nothing on the menu is out of context, pretentious or gratuitous. You won't see words like "sous vide" or "emulsion." Yet when a dish arrives, you can tell that each aspect has been carefully considered. The colors are vibrant (a natural result of using the best fresh local ingredients), the flavors are balanced and the portions hearty.

When his ahi toast arrived at the table, his daughter Ariana followed seconds after with a glass of rosé she felt would pair nicely. I think people on the mainland get to see vibrant, deep red tuna like this only if it's been treated with chemicals, which this ahi most assuredly had not. The peppered and seared fish sat on neat toast rounds, which Mark makes in-house with whole grains and crusts with flax seed ("Because, you know, it's good for you," he grins). Underneath is his signature edamame hummus. He finishes the dish with local micro greens (from Monica at Napili Flo Farms), yellow and red tomato, julienned basil and aged balsamic.

There's enough punch here to trick the mind into thinking you're eating a steak, yet the salad, tomatoes and edamame are bright and counterbalance the weight of the tuna medallions. The acid from the balsamic and the salt & pepper, plus the hearty homemade bread, tie the dish together eloquently.

Settling into a table at one of Mark Ellman's Maui restaurants is like coming home. There's a warmth and comfort not easily achieved in the dining world. The lack of pretension paired with great food and drink makes for a special meal every time. I think you would really appreciate coming here, Mom.

With love, Bill

Mark Ellman

Chef and restaurateur Mark Ellman is what I consider to be the unsuspecting Hawaii chef. Mark cut his teeth in California, making a name for himself and earning a loyal following, which, in turn, seemed to follow him to Hawaii. Those relationships, strengthened perhaps by the distance over the Pacific and a love for rock 'n' roll, helped elevate Mark to the top of the field in the late 1980s and 1990s on Maui. He's still filling every seat in his Maui restaurant empire, this many years later. And with good reason.

Mark met his wife, Judy, in a Calabasas, California, restaurant where she was a bartender and he worked on the line. They fell in love and decided if they could open a successful restaurant together, their love would last eternal. A successful Italian eatery proved their dedication to both the business and one another. So they set sails . . . for Colorado. While the mountains proved lovely, the pair were destined for warmth. They set course for Maui, hoisted the sails again, and hove to.

The Ellmans opened Avalon in 1987 in downtown Lahaina, feeding everyone from celebrity rock stars to restaurant industry devotees and in-the-know tourists. Mark took to Hawaiian fusion cuisine, and was able to make friends with a number of local chefs across the islands . . . 11 others, to be exact. They went on to form the storied "Hawaii Regional Cuisine" movement and spearheaded the printing of a book that featured a chef in every chapter. (A novel concept!)

In 1998 the pair sold Avalon to focus on a few taco stands they launched, called Maui Tacos, mainly to satisfy their craving for Mexican from their Los Angeles days. Mark incorporated the business and eventually opened shops on Oahu, in California, and on Fifth Avenue, in New York City. They also opened a casual pasta eatery called Penne Pasta.

Mark truly hit his stride in 2005 when he opened Mala Ocean Tavern, on the Mala Wharf, just outside of hopping Lahaina town. Positioned right on the water, they began serving fresh and organic seafood with Hawaii and Mediterranean influences. Mala quickly earned a devout following from the locals, which in turn put it on the radar of guidebooks and foodies around the world, who descended hungrily. Mark and Judy now employed their two lovely daughters, Ariana and Michelle, who helped streamline the family vision and enable their next two ventures: Honu Seafood & Pizza and Frida's Mexican Beach House.

With friends and business partners like Shep Gordon, Alice Cooper and Clint Eastwood, the Ellmans have no shortage of excitement buzzing around their homey and familial island restaurant empire.

Ahi Bruschetta

AHI BRUSCHETTA is one of those mash-up, mind-bendingly simple dishes that just absolutely rocks your world. Slices of seared tuna on toast: Simple enough, right? Yet the combination of sashimi grade and seared rare tuna steaks with dense whole grain bread and the fluffy, flavor of packed edamame purée is just the ultimate pairing. The aged vinegar and micro greens add an acidic element as well as color and that peppery crunch only fresh micro greens can deliver.

Heat a large sauté pan with the olive oil and sear the ahi tuna rare, approximately 3 seconds each side. Place in the refrigerator to cool quickly.

Slice the bread into ¼-inch pieces coated with the clarified butter. Grill them over an open flame, or toast if easier.

Edamame Purée
Blanche the edamame beans, then place in a food processor. Add the olive oil, rice wine vinegar and salt and pepper to taste as the food processor is blending.

To serve, spread the edamame purée on top of the grilled bread. Next, place slices of alternating yellow and red tomatoes and salt and pepper tomatoes to taste. On top of tomato slices, place 2 slices of seared rare ahi tuna, and top with 1 tablespoon of the basil and salt and pepper to taste.

Top the ahi with 1 tablespoon of micro greens, and drizzle the olive oil and balsamic vinegar on the greens.

Serves 4

2 tablespoons olive oil

4 (8-ounce) blocks fresh ahi tuna, sashimi grade

1 loaf dense, flax seed bread, or other dense whole-grain bread

Clarified butter

Freshly ground black pepper

Edamame Purée

1 pound edamame, peeled and thawed

1 cup extra virgin olive oil

¼ rice wine vinegar

Salt and pepper

Ripe yellow and red tomatoes, sliced

Salt and pepper to taste

4 tablespoons basil, julienne

4 tablespoons micro greens

Extra virgin olive oil, for drizzling

Villa Manodori balsamic vinegar, for drizzling

Dear Mom,

I want to write to you about a relative newcomer to Hawaii's culinary scene, Lee Anne Wong. You would appreciate her competitive nature, on vivid display in *Top Chef*, the elimination-style cooking show that pits a dozen chefs against each other. She made it to the top four chefs during the show's very first season, before being ousted but remained a crowd favorite.

Nearly a decade after her appearance, she moved from New York to Hawaii. She was likely one of many chefs who come out for a vacation or a culinary festival and fall in love with the culture—as well as the fresh ingredients from our farms and sea.

She opened a breakfast place called Koko Head Cafe; within days of opening there were lines around the corner right up until closing time. There still are.

On the heels of her success in the breakfast world, she opened Hale Ohuna, a full bar and restaurant that featured her take on traditional Hawaiian fare, jazzed up the way a savvy

chef would. All this in a trendy environment with dim lighting and even a secret room for those who want to appreciate a quiet dinner. With Hale Ohuna, Lee Anne wasn't mimicking the foods of Hawaii here; rather, she gave us her take on the flavors of classic Hawaiian dishes and paired them with an impressive menu of American and Japanese whiskeys.

We Tobins have always been fans of Lee Anne's breakfast menu at Koko Head Cafe, which is both simple and stellar. She has a number of omelettes with interesting ingredients (a French omelette made extra sultry with cream whipped into the egg batter) as well as an umami mushroom egg plate, the flavors of which are almost indescribable. Sweet and salty, it is an explosion of flavor. She also features a different dumpling every day—perhaps a nod to her Chinese heritage. I don't think I've seen the same dumpling special twice in the dozens of times I've eaten at Koko Head Cafe.

Where I think Lee Anne really shines is in her take on traditional breakfast jazzed up in *Top Chef* fashion. Both me and the kids are bonkers for her French toast. Although she swears to secrecy on the full recipe, I'll do my best to describe it.

The square bread is just thick enough to soak up the sweet, eggy batter, yet it stays light and fluffy. The crust is covered in Corn Flakes. Yes, the very same cereal we all grew up with. I suspect she adds some ingredients to the crushed flakes before dipping the bread into the cereal and pan frying.

This is a prime example of a great chef who takes something we might have eaten a thousand times, alters it just enough to shift our perspective on it while keeping its identity. To put it over the top, Lee Anne adorns her French toast with two pieces of thick-cut bacon; its salty, fatty essence is absorbed into the top of the toast. The crunchy texture of the Corn Flakes crust creates a wow factor that I've really come to love. However, for me, it's that essence of corn that ties into my memories.

I tell people here that the hardest job I ever had was detasseling corn. What's common knowledge to a kid growing up surrounded by Nebraska cornfields, others might not know much about. Like the fact that nearly all the corn we eat is a hybrid of two varietals. I relish in explaining to people here on the islands how farmers will crossbreed two varieties of corn to craft a sustainable and flourishing crop. This is a natural process, very different from genetic modification. When I tell friends that this hybridization entailed walking along miles and miles of corn rows to remove the tassels—plant by plant—they're astonished. I guess my summer job was pretty different from most people's!

I did that job for two seasons, walking miles a day. It was exhausting (and now done by machine), but even so, I still love the taste of corn.

So sure, there's a crunch factor to Lee Anne's French toast, but for me there's also a bit of nostalgia. It's funny how the best dishes bring us back to something from our past.

Although Hale Ohuna didn't remain open for long, Lee Anne's success came from the dishes that connected with people's emotions on a visceral level. Mom, I'm not sure how to stress this, but someone not from Hawaii coming to the islands and opening a Hawaiian fare restaurant—especially a dinner restaurant as opposed to a plate lunch stand or something more casual—takes serious gumption.

I believe Lee Anne's outgoing demeanor (she walks around the dining room saying hello to patrons at every breakfast service at Koko Head Cafe) and her media savvy have really helped her become a success in the islands. She's giving local diners exactly what they want: unpretentious, high-quality, affordable food in a fun and engaging atmosphere.

We're lucky to have this nationally recognized (and still rising) star in the culinary world drawing the attention of young foodies around the country. To have her bringing the spotlight to Honolulu is *big* for Hawaii. I'm confident there's more great stuff yet to come from Lee Anne Wong.

With love, *Bill*

Lee Anne Wong

Lee Anne Wong has walked an unusual path in the culinary field, one that wound its way to the islands in 2012, when she opened a sensational breakfast cafe. She's been making waves ever since. Lee Anne had never lived in Hawaii before packing up her knives in a Queens, New York, apartment and relocating.

Lee Anne is perhaps best known as one of the four finalists in the first season of *Top Chef*, Bravo's competitive cooking show. After the first season, Lee Anne impressed the producers enough for them to sign her on as a culinary producer for the next four seasons. Her tasks ranged from sourcing ingredients for contestants to determining their budgets and equipment limitations. She blogged about the show and hosted a fan webcast, which was very popular thanks to the show's meteoric success.

Lee Anne began her studies at the Fashion Institute of America but switched to the French Culinary Institute, where she not only graduated but served as director of event operations for many years. It's safe to say she has a knack for impressing her superiors.

Settling into a back alley locale off a main Oahu avenue in Kaimuki, Lee Anne's Koko Head Cafe had lines outside the door from the day it opened until, well, there are still lines. She serves an amazing range of brunch items from a relatively tiny kitchen (yet another win for the *Top Chef* competitor), packing a lot of punch into a simple-sounding menu. If Lee Anne peers out from behind the line in her signature multicolored trucker hat and recognizes you as a return customer, you might find yourself with a "Coffee and Doughnuts" treat on your table (oh, that Kona coffee cream anglaise!). If not, just order it. Every time.

Having published a lovely cookbook of her own, Lee Anne has a rotating section of the menu dedicated to dumplings, another of her passions. She's done years of R&D, plus a fair amount of global galavanting to perfect over one hundred styles of dumpling. And the cornucopia of fresh ingredients, ranched meats and local fish in Hawaii has been a boon to everyone who has an opportunity to taste those gooey pockets of savory goodness. The team working to develop this book would sometimes hold breakfast production meetings at Lee Anne's cafe, lingering long enough to justify a dessert, then meet again for lunch and order dumplings. What can I say? We're spoiled in Hawaii.

Koko Moco

LOCO MOCO is one of the most ubiquitous contemporary Hawaiian dishes: A hamburger patty on top of white rice, smothered in brown gravy and topped with a fried egg. The first loco moco originated on Big Island (Hawaii) back in 1949. At Koko Head Cafe, our "Koko Moco" uses 100 percent local Hawaiian grass-fed beef for our hamburger patties. We take high-quality sushi rice and press it into a skillet with seasoned garlic oil to give the rice a lightly crunchy crust. Our savory mushroom gravy is made from scratch and is a meatless wonder on its own! We top it all off with a sunny-side up fried local egg, thinly sliced scallions, sesame seeds, togarashi spice, and tempura fried kimchi.

Beef Patties
In a small bowl combine the shoyu, Worcestershire, salt and black pepper, mixing well. Pour over the ground beef and massage with your hands until well mixed, being careful to not overwork the meat. Form the beef into four 6-ounce patties, about 4 inches in diameter and ½ inch thick. Refrigerate covered until needed.

Garlic Oil
Combine the oil and garlic cloves in a small pan or pot. Simmer on low heat until the garlic begins to turn golden and the oil becomes fragrant, about 20 to 30 minutes. Allow the oil to cool to room temperature. Remove the garlic and save for another use.

Savory Mushroom Gravy
Remove the rehydrated shiitake mushrooms from the soaking liquid, squeezing out excess liquid. Reserve the mushroom water. Remove the stems from the rehydrated shiitakes, set aside. Slice the mushrooms into ¼-inch thick slices, set aside.

In a medium saucepan, melt the butter over medium-high heat and sauté the onions for 5 minutes until they begin to soften, stirring often with a wooden spoon. Add the minced garlic and cook for 1 minute more. Sprinkle the flour over the mixture and stir well until incorporated; it will become thick like a dough. Slowly add in the mushroom soaking liquid, stirring out any lumps (use a whisk) until all of the liquid has been added. Continue to whisk and cook over medium heat for 3 minutes. Add the Maggi seasoning, mushroom soy sauce, sugar and black pepper.

Combine the shiitake mushroom stems and the cremini mushroom trimmings and stems with the cream. Add the minced sage, bring to a simmer over medium-high heat. Reduce to low heat and cook until the stems are tender, about 5 minutes. Purée the cream and mushroom mixture on high in a blender until it is a smooth purée. Add the purée to the mushroom gravy pot.

Continued

Beef Patties
1 tablespoon shoyu (soy sauce)
1 tablespoon Worcestershire sauce
Salt
½ teaspoon ground black pepper
1½ pounds high-quality grass-fed ground beef

Garlic Oil
1 cup vegetable oil
12 large cloves peeled garlic, smashed/crushed

Savory Mushroom Gravy
1 cup dried shiitake mushrooms soaked overnight in 4 cups water
6 tablespoons butter
1 cup finely minced yellow onions
1 tablespoon garlic, minced
⅔ cup all purpose flour
3 tablespoons Maggi seasoning
3 tablespoons mushroom soy sauce
½ tablespoon sugar
1 teaspoon ground black pepper
3 cups cremini mushrooms, quartered, trimmed, stems reserved
1 cup heavy cream
1 tablespoon dried sage or 3 tablespoons fresh sage, minced

Oil for sautéing mushrooms

Koko Moco
4 cups cooked white rice
1 teaspoon finely minced garlic
4 (6-ounce) beef patties
Salt and pepper
4 large eggs
Garlic oil

1 green onion, minced
Togarashi
Toasted sesame seeds

Bring the mushroom gravy to a boil, whisking until smooth. Check for seasoning and adjust as necessary. Purée the gravy in the blender on high in small batches (be careful to only fill the blender pitcher halfway and keep the lid held tightly on with a toweled hand). Return the finished gravy to a clean pot.

In a large sauté pan, heat up a few tablespoons of oil over high heat and add the quartered cremini mushrooms. Season with salt and pepper. Cook the mushrooms for 2 to 3 minutes, stirring often. Add the sliced shiitake mushrooms to the pan and cook, stir frying vigorously for another 3 minutes until all of the mushrooms are cooked and tender. Drain on paper towels then add the cooked mushrooms to the mushroom gravy. Keep warm or refrigerate until needed.

Koko Moco

Heat four 6-inch skillets (or a small 6- to 8-inch nonstick pan) on high heat until they begin to lightly smoke. If using a small nonstick pan, you will need to fry four batches of rice, or you can use a large nonstick pan and cut the rice in quarters once finished. Add a tablespoon of oil to the skillets and press 1 cup of rice into the bottom of each skillet. Reduce heat to medium-high and cook until lightly golden brown. Add a ¼ teaspoon of fresh minced garlic on the top of the rice and gently stir in. Season the rice with salt.

Separately: Season the beef patties with salt and pepper. Grill or griddle the beef patties to desired temperature.

Fry the eggs individually sunny side up in a nonstick pan using garlic oil to fry, season with salt and pepper.

Warm the mushroom gravy in a small pot. To assemble, place the cooked burger patty on top of the seasoned garlic rice. Ladle a generous portion of gravy over the burger (½ to 1 cup). Top with a fried egg and garnish with sliced green onion, togarashi, salt and toasted sesame seeds. Serve immediately.

Serves 4

Dear Mom,

I'm not sure I've ever told you in person, but I have you to thank for the tactics I use in my own parenting. One of them comes to mind today. You probably wouldn't be surprised to learn that I'm pretty involved in Toby's school as well as Cub Scouts and other activities. You and Dad, regardless of how busy the weekdays were on the farm, always carved out time to get involved with our interests, partaking whenever you could. In fact, I can't think of a single event you missed, even after you became a full-time registered nurse. All those times you were at my sporting events and school functions were, upon reflection, the most memorable times of my childhood. I've acknowledged that, and I'm trying to do the same with my three boys—your grandsons. I know if you could, you'd be here doing the same.

Toby's school held a science fair a few weeks ago. Before the fair, he casually asked me whether I had any ideas to wow his classmates. Naturally, my mind turned to food. You have to remember, Hawaii is such a melting pot of cultures, which brings both good and awkward nuances to everyday life. But the one constant is that each culture here seems to relish in the flavor variations and oddities of the others. The saying is true: You can learn the most about a culture by what they put on their dinner plate. Hawaii is no exception.

I put Toby in the car, and we went on a treasure hunt; we needed to find a specific candy from my childhood days. And it's all because of one very avant-garde Maui chef, Jojo Vasquez.

Let's back up a few months: Tracy and I had taken the boys to Maui over the holidays, and we snuck out for an adult night. Jojo was the chef at a restaurant called the Banyan Tree, in the Ritz-Carlton at Kapalua. The meal was exquisite, all served on an incredibly romantic bluff overlooking the ocean. We could hear the waves crashing a few hundred yards away, and every now and again feel the warm, salty breeze. We were relishing the respite from parenting.

I could rhapsodize about nearly every dish that Jojo sent out to our table, but I'll share with you the last: an impossibly light, bittersweet chocolate mousse cake with a papaya salsa and a dollop of housemade dulce du leche ice cream. The plate was painted (literally, with a paint brush) with a vibrant green avocado cream. The dish had what appeared to be large sea salt crystals shimmering around the plate: The waiter instructed us to "make sure you get some of those in each bite" before smiling cryptically and walking off. The textures came together so effortlessly, yet I could tell each element of this dessert took time to master—and Jojo had done it impeccably. And then . . . a series of small explosions detonated in my mouth. Had I just broken a tooth?

No! The crystals were dark chocolate-flavored Pop Rocks—the 1980s candy that crackles in your mouth. Here was a chef at the helm of a fine eatery in a Ritz-Carlton, serving us eloquent fare course after course. And then he finishes up with this playful, laugh-out-loud addition to an already delicious dessert. It had so much subtext, as if he were saying, "Yes, I've got mad chef skills but, hey, lighten up! Food is fun." At least that's how I interpreted it. (You're probably laughing at this idea of a chef trying to send "a message" to his diners through ingredients.) At the very least, it woke us up. On the stroll back to our hotel room, I found myself rethinking a lot of my favorite dishes throughout the years, how another feature could be worked into them.

Jojo's passion for food and its subtexts might be unparalleled in Hawaii—or anywhere I've been. Since that first encounter, I've tasted more of his food and learned that what he puts on a plate is more like a personal memoir—his story, his passion, his connection to the place where he lives—than a mere technical rehearsal of what culinary chops he acquired from other chefs. His food is an incredible experience I hope to share with you some day.

Back to Toby and his science project. I sought out the only place on Oahu that had Pop Rocks at the time and let Toby and his friends taste them back at the house. They were giddy! It was a blast to watch. I was transported back to the days of rummaging for spare change in the car seats (and everywhere else) just so I could head to the candy shop in our small Nebraska town. And here, on a hillside in Hawaii, smack in the middle of the Pacific Ocean (and thirty-something years later), my oldest son is having the same giddy fun as I had.

And so we incorporated them into a lemonade smoothie.

Let's just say that "The Great Honolulu Science Fair Pop Rocks Experiment" will go down as a success during research and development, but the success mostly ended there. The memory he'll take with him is us in our kitchen, laughing uncontrollably with his buddies as we tasted our way through a rainbow of Pop Rocks flavors. The judges didn't exactly see the value of the experience—nor detect much of a science angle. But it was a great lesson I was able to pass onto my son: Taste and experience is completely subjective. You can't judge anyone for his or her opinion. Whether he intended the lesson or not, I have Jojo Vasquez to thank for that one.

With love, Bill

Jojo Vasquez

Chef Jojo Vasquez might be among the least talked about of Hawaii's top chefs, but he is in my opinion one of the most spectacular to watch. Jojo combines his analytical, science-oriented mind, extensive training and the influences of his Filipino heritage. *Iron Chef* Masaharu Morimoto selected Jojo to help him compete on national television and serve as his right-hand man when opening new restaurant locations.

Jojo ascended the ranks in multiple Ritz-Carlton kitchens, from Chicago to California and Hawaii. He attended Kendall Culinary Academy in Chicago, where he grew up, which could explain his affinity for life in Hawaii. The warmth of the tropics—as well as the farmers and culinary community he's connected with here—have brought him to Maui time and again.

"The direct relationships with the farmers is what keeps me going for menu changes and inspiration," Jojo says. "I mean, I was immersed in produce in California, where most of America's greens are grown. But I never met or spoke with a farmer; it was all trucked in. Here I can feature a farmer or a single ingredient because it was hand-delivered by that farmer. I can use that to really tell a story on the plate."

Jojo took things to another level when he met a local farmer in Napili (less than two miles from Plantation House restaurant at Kapalua, Maui, where he runs the kitchen). Monica Bogar has installed simplified aquaponics systems on every usable inch of land around her home, which churn out impeccable micro greens. Her systems are completely sustainable, powered by water and tilapia. (She's so passionate about aquaponics that she regularly sets up home systems for chefs or budding agricultural enthusiasts, including Jojo.)

Watching Jojo pull a few watercress shoots out of the water tray and sample them, I share in his delight as a broad smile illuminates his face. "I know you've tasted local, mass farmed watercress on Oahu, and it's good," he says. "But it's not this good! Totally different feel and flavor."

His excitement continues to grow when he and Monica talk about what she can grow with aquaponics (nearly any shallow-rooted plant). Later, Jojo shares that he can plan out menu items a season or two in advance because of the quick growth of aquaponic produce and the flexibility to plant different and new crops. Jojo likens the experience to creating his own almanac. "It's the future," he says, noting that he often brings his kids along to learn from Monica.

"It's like a dream, to be able to have this. It's like a science lab. And it's bringing me to the next level as a chef," Jojo says, adding that he can introduce diners to things they likely haven't seen before.

I've known Jojo since his pre-Morimoto days, when he helmed Banyan Tree at the Ritz-Carlton Kapalua (where he blew our minds with the Pop Rocks dish, which you can read about in the preceding pages). He's cooked at Aspen Food & Wine Festival, Pebble Beach, Cape Cod, in Russia for an entire season (yes, it was winter) and on Oahu. He's never been so happy to be staying put on Maui.

"I cook for where I work," Jojo says. "At Banyan I had big budget and a diverse, well-traveled crowd, so the Pop Rocks thing worked. With Morimoto I cooked Japanese. Here, I cook mostly for golfers who don't want delicate or fussy food. But I have evolved them in my four years here—they are eating better. I'm proud of that."

Monchong with Watercress, Green Beans and Tamarind-Coriander Broth

CHEF JOJO Vasquez is a master at melding worlds. Raised in Chicago with Filipino heritage, Vasquez felt an immediate connection with Hawaii when he and his wife honeymooned on Maui. In this dish, Vasquez makes use of prized local monchong fillet, floats it in a sauce that nods to his heritage and finishes the dish with watercress harvested in an aquaponic system less than two miles from his restaurant. It's a beautiful representation of both Maui and Vasquez's dedication to the seamless integration of varied flavor profiles.

In a pot on medium heat, toast coriander seeds until fragrant. Add the oil, onion, garlic and ginger then sauté until tender. Add chili flakes and deglaze with the patis until dry. Add the tamarind paste and tomato paste and lightly toast for 1 minute to extract the flavor.

Cover the pot with the chopped tomatoes and water. Season with salt and pepper then bring to a boil. When you reach a boil, reduce to a simmer and bruise a bunch of cilantro with the back of your knife to release the aromatic scent. Add the cilantro to the simmering broth and cook for 15 to 20 minutes. Check seasoning, then add beans and cook until tender; about 8 minutes. Remove from the heat.

Heat a sauté pan, season the fish with salt and pepper and sear on both sides for about 4 minutes each or until cooked through. Arrange the cooked fish in a large bowl and pour enough broth to cover the fish. Top with the watercress, along with more cilantro and fresh tomatoes for garnish.

Serve family style with white rice and a San Miguel beer. Enjoy!

Serves 4

Tamarind-Coriander Broth

5 tablespoons coriander seeds

1 tablespoon grape seed oil

1 onion, diced

5 cloves garlic, chopped

1 small piece ginger, chopped

1 teaspoon chili flakes

2 tablespoons patis (Filipino fish sauce)

2 tablespoons tamarind paste

1 teaspoon tomato paste

2 tomatoes, seeded and chopped

8 cups (2 quarts) water

Salt and black pepper to taste

Handful of cilantro, bruised

1 pound green beans

4 pieces, 6 ounces each monchong* fillet, or any fresh Hawaiian fish

Salt and pepper

½ pound fresh watercress

*Monchong is in the pomfret family of bottom-dwelling fish. It's an oily white fish and can be replaced with anything similar from your local market. Fresh is best.

Dear Mom,

I feel compelled to share an experience with you that absolutely blew my mind. Seriously, I'm in complete awe.

Geoge Mavrothalassitis—called Chef Mavro here—is the kind of a chef who can turn the dining experience into a dance. His masterful platings are poetry; his restaurant is a theater of culinary delight. He has the power to take a meal—or even just a single ingredient—to a transcendent level.

I say with genuine certainty that Mavro is Hawaii's best example of what fine-dining should be. Heading into Chef Mavro restaurant is an event. You dress up, maybe push aside the row of aloha shirts in your closet and grab that dress shirt you've been saving for a special occasion. You feel a little better about yourself the day you're headed into his restaurant. It's very likely you'll leave having eaten something you've never tasted before. And it will be fantastic.

Here at Mavro I came to understand for the first time the dance that's involved in elevated restaurants. It's a choreography that includes a seamless flow of service, idyllic lighting, an array of flavors. All of it is the confluence of a multisensory experience—nothing is disconnected or dissonant; it's all somehow woven together, a singular work of art.

Chef Mavro is located in an unexpected place, a somewhat gritty avenue, miles away from the palm-lined beaches and crystal clear waters that everyone associates with life in Hawaii. Maybe that's a good thing; there are no distractions. And yet, here, you can truly savor nuances like the fresh shaving of seasonal truffle that Mavro imports from a specific village in France.

What really blows my mind—as I started off saying—is that Mavro sends out only the most impeccable dishes, creations that could rightfully receive a James Beard Award (which, of course, they have), and then he offers to shave a truffle over it. There are chefs the world over who consider their diners blessed to have a few slivers of truffle on their lobster pasta or what have you. Then there's Mavro, who offers it as a garnish to an already-jaw dropping plate of culinary wizardry. Amazing.

I have some news, Mom, that might make you proud. I've been named chairman of the Hawaii Restaurant Association. In this role, my relationship with Mavro has evolved in a most unlikely way. I started out sending handwritten cards to several chefs, often just "thank you's" for hosting a dinner or a note expressing a thought I had regarding their significance in the Hawaii food community. During my first year as chairman, I would end each card with the phrase: "There's more that unites us than divides us." In one note to Mavro, I thanked him for being a wonderful representation of Hawaii. For showing us what was possible in the hands of one, great master.

This opened the door to an ongoing friendship with his wife, Donna Jung, who is first seat violinist in the symphony that is Chef Mavro restaurant. She is his PR, marketing and "everything" gal. She has all the front-of-house know-how and presents him exquisitely (especially as English is his third or maybe fourth language!). They have an admirable balance to their partnership—and the national awards to prove it.

If you want to know about ingredients, Mom, two things come to mind here. There's a product called sea asparagus in Hawaii. It's a crunchy, salty little stalk of deep green that looks like a tiny asparagus—just like the ones you grew in the garden on our farm—but it's harvested from a saltwater aquaponics farm on Oahu. Mavro uses them to add alkalinity without using salt. It becomes both a flavor enhancer and a garnish while also being a component of the dish. This is just one small example of how this chef researches his ingredients deeply. Sometimes I think he's more a mathematician or scientist than chef; he calculates what parts per plate will equal an astonishing sum, or how to treat a Hawaiian product with a French technique that leaves diners with something both astoundingly beautiful and delicious.

On a recent visit to Chef Mavro, I treated Tracy to a special sustainable caviar presentation the chef offered. Although I had no idea what we were in for, our previous experiences here led me to believe it would be spectacular. It didn't disappoint.

After our first glass of bubbly, out wheeled a cart. The server removed a cloth like a magician unveiling the box in which he'll saw someone in half, and under it was a gigantic block of ice. It had three holes perfectly carved into its surface. The server showed us three ornate caviar tins; one from the Baltic, one from Washington State and one from northeastern Canada. Mavro had researched how each of these caviar producers gives back to the environment, keeping the quality high while still maintaining sustainable fish egg farm practices.

We were then served eloquent toast points, crème fraîche, chopped onion and other garnishes. A pair of oyster shell spoons were our utensils. Tracy went from, "Oh, I'm not sure caviar is for me" to, "This is so much fun!" And just like that—another magical moment conjured by Mavro.

I hope to take you to Chef Mavro on your next visit. While I'm sure it will be overwhelming and wild for you, I feel like you'll understand how he fits into the complicated, delicious fabric of Hawaii fine dining. You'll adore this dance.

With love, Bill

George Mavrothalassitis

Chef Mavro is, to me, the best chef on the islands. Sometimes I don't know how he maintains such a high level of quality and manages to stay in business; the level of product he uses, the locations from which he sources ingredients and his ability to use it all . . . it's astonishing. Yet it shows in his accolades. He has a James Beard Award. He's earned AAA's Five Diamond status every year since 2008; Gayot and Fodors have put him in their "Top 40" and "Top 10 Seafood" restaurants worldwide lists at various times. These awards go on and on (you can see many of them hanging in the foyer of his King Street restaurant). Regardless of what others have bestowed upon him, he simply orchestrates the most engaging and memorable dining experience from start to finish.

George Mavrothalassitis was born in the port town of Marseilles, the capital of Provence in France. Raised around the fishmongers there, he owned a gourmet restaurant before moving onto Restaurant La Presqu'ile in Cassis. He relocated to Hawaii and helmed Halekulani's La Mer kitchen before opening his signature eatery, the rest is history. Alongside his wife and marketing manager Donna Jung, they have hosted dignitaries and celebrities while maintaining a loyal local following.

Mavro has guided burgeoning culinary talent (as well as front of house) who are indoctrinated into his process. He treats his staff as equals, soliciting their input on select dishes. He isn't a maniacal "my way or the highway" type; he knows there's plenty to learn in life and cooking, and the collaboration isn't limited to the kitchen.

An aspect of his practices that's always impressed me is the way each of his seasonal menus comes together. Each quarter, as the menu items are finalized, Mavro sits the entire staff down at two long tables during their closed day. Each dish from the forthcoming menu is served alongside a selection of wines for pairing. The entire Mavro team votes on their favorite pairings, and the winners are the wines that make it to the final, printed pairings menu.

The idea that Mavro, as chef and owner, plus his wine director, will solicit the feedback from the entire staff exhibits two things: An unparalleled trust in the people he hires and employs, as well as their dedication to making the restaurant a success. I'm sure we've all worked in places where the top brass wouldn't bat an eye at an underling, let alone ask their opinion. And here, Mavro's reputation and standings in the global press can be traced to a pairing his whole team devised. It's nothing short of impressive.

Day-Boat Catch Poached Fillet with Sago-Coconut Nage, Thai Herbs, "Pousse-Pierre" and Lime Froth

IF YOU WERE a fish swimming in Hawaiian waters, you'd be hard pressed to find a better way to end your life than inside the kitchen at Chef Mavro. The manner in which Chef treats his ingredients, elevating them to otherworldly morsels of delight, it just seems to be the most civilized way to go. Here, Mavro bathes a snapper fillet in a delightful coconut nage that is light and airy, making use of Thai flavors. The crisp, salty sea asparagus is both an artist's addition to the visual nature of the plate, but also a welcome flavor burst. Finally, the lime froth may seem decadent and over-the-top . . . because it is. And it's perfect.

Preheat an oven to 250°F.

Sago-Coconut Nage
Infuse the curry leaves, ginger and lemongrass in nage for 2 hours. Strain the liquid and reserve some liquid for the lime froth. Add the coconut cream, sago, Thai basil, and toasted coconut. Season with sea salt and white pepper.

Poached Fish
Season the fish with sea salt and white pepper. Brush parchment paper with extra virgin olive oil. Place the fish on the parchment paper and cover with some of the infused nage, reserving some for serving. Cover with another piece of oiled parchment paper and place in the preheated oven for 6 minutes or until the fish is done.

Sea Asparagus "Pousse-Pierre"
Wash the sea asparagus in cold water and remove any discolored pieces. Dry the sea asparagus. Heat a large sauté pan with olive oil and sauté the sea asparagus for 30 seconds. Season with sea salt and white pepper.

Lime Froth
Heat the infused nage in a small sauce pot with lime juice. Add the soy lecithin and season with sea salt and white pepper. Simmer for 5 minutes or until the soy lecithin dissolves. Froth the liquid using an aerolatte.

To serve, pour the remaining sago-coconut nage in a large soup plate. Place the fish in the center of the soup plate. Put the sea asparagus on top of the poached fish. Spoon the lime froth on the sea asparagus.

Serves 10

Sago-Coconut Nage
- 1 dozen curry leaves
- 1 ounce fresh ginger, peeled and smashed
- 3 stalks lemongrass, bruised
- 3 cups nage
- 1½ cups coconut cream
- ½ cup cooked baby sago
- 2 tablespoons Thai basil, chiffonade
- 2 tablespoons toasted unsweetened coconut flakes
- Sea salt and freshly ground white pepper to taste

10 (5-ounce) fillets fresh local fish

Sea Asparagus "Pousse-Pierre"
- 4 ounces sea asparagus
- 1 teaspoon extra virgin olive oil
- Sea salt and freshly ground white pepper to taste

Lime Froth
- ½ cup (reserved) sago-coconut nage
- 1 tablespoon lime juice
- ½ teaspoon soy lecithin
- Sea salt and freshly ground white pepper to taste

Dear Mom,

We've recently hired a new chef here at Tiki's, and I'm feeling rather blessed to have not only found, but befriended him and now have him leading our culinary team. Ronnie Nasuti, mark my words, will be the catalyst for taking Tiki's Grill & Bar to new heights. He's an Italian guy from suburban Boston who has lived in these islands for more than 25 years. Hiring Chef Ronnie was a pretty amazing experience for me in the restaurant business, Mom. And I'd like to share with you the events that unfolded for it to happen, as they were part serendipity, part strategic and a whole lot of good energy coming together. Here's the story:

I had just let our chef go—I had thought he was really bringing the team down, and I felt relieved when I realized I had the sense to make a substantial change that would better the Tiki's organization. So I put out an ad on Craigslist that read, "If you are Chef Mavro, I will pay you $250,000 to come work at Tiki's and run our kitchen. If you're Alan Wong, I'll pay $200,000. If you are Kevin Hanney, I've got $175,000 for you. For Ronnie Nasuti I'll pay $150,000 . . ." and I went on down the line with a few more chefs. A few days later Ronnie called me, said he wanted to talk.

(As a side note: Alan Wong every once in a while takes a comical jab at me asking why I thought he was valued less than Chef Mavro! Some restaurant humor . . .)

Anyway, as Ronnie was coming in to talk to me, I realized something: Of the list I posted in the ad, Ronnie was the only chef who didn't own his own restaurant. I had noticed his hard work and how much he elevated Roy's kitchen—where he had worked for over 10 years—as well as at food events around town.

Ronnie had never gotten to build out his very own kitchen. Helming Roy's for a decade, he'd run the show with a staff that was selected by a management team. Since Roy doesn't spend a lot of time in his kitchens, even though he is the face of that brand, Roy's is a streamlined operation with one man—Roy—at the helm. I sensed Ronnie was ready for change, so . . . we worked something out and I hired him on the spot.

And it was pretty seamless. Ronnie now was able to groom the staff he selected. He told me our prior kitchen operated like the Wild West, with no rules or structure. He started making changes immediately and all for the better.

We started casting the spotlight on him from the onset; adding his name first and Tiki's second at food shows, doing articles on him in the local and national media. In reality—yet not in "reality TV"—95 percent of chefs would choose to let their food speak for them, shrugging off requests to be cast in the limelight. But Ronnie started taking all of it in stride, understanding that it was an evolution for him, personally, as well as a way to get some great attention for his food at our restaurant. We made him our face man, leveraging his great pedigree with a class act operation like Roy's to show that a Waikiki bar can churn out respectable fare, too.

Business has been increasing and feedback on our food has been overwhelmingly positive. This has led to more parties and events, which is wonderful business for us. And it's also let us spread our wings with things like live music, a cocktail program, beer and winemaker dinners and more.

I'm super excited for you to meet Ronnie, Mom. You're going to be proud at the way we've evolved Tiki's with his leadership.

With love, Bill

Ronnie Nasuti

Tiki's Grill & Bar Executive Chef Ronnie Nasuti has been working in and around kitchens his entire life. The youngest of four in an Italian-American family from the Boston suburbs, Chef Ronnie recalls with great enthusiasm his father making "sauce" and meatballs in their modest kitchen for hours on Sundays, all while belting out opera. Although he passed away when Ronnie was eight years old, his mother took the reigns as the homemaker and breadwinner. Ronnie jumped into his first restaurant job at thirteen, washing dishes.

"I knew then, in eighth grade, that I wanted to cook," Nasuti says.

By seventeen, he was the kitchen manager of a classic Northern Italian restaurant there, where he assisted the chef/owner, learning the ropes of cooking as well as owning a business. He finished four years of culinary arts in vocational high school, continuing on at Les Dames Escoffier Society followed by a culinary apprenticeship.

He moved to Hawaii at twenty and almost immediately heard about "the buzz" surrounding Roy Yamaguchi's new fine-dining concept. Knowing it would offer him the best education in island fare, he set his sights and landed at Roy's Park Bistro in Waikiki, learning every station including pastry. He moved over to the flagship Roy's in Hawaii Kai, training under Roy himself, as well as Gordon Hopkins and Jacqueline Lau. He was elevated to sous chef at Roy's Poipu Bar & Grill in Kauai, only to return to Hawaii Kai as executive sous chef. Following a five year departure to Chez Michel in Honolulu, he returned to Roy's Hawaii Kai once again, this time as executive chef—a position he held for ten years.

A passion for travel and new experiences led him to meeting Bill Tobin, the owner of Tiki's Grill & Bar, who hired Ronnie to take over their high volume Waikiki kitchen. In addition to tightening the reigns and streamlining operations, Ronnie has been able to stretch his wings as well. In 2011, he launched a periodic winemakers' dinner, which features a custom menu planned entirely by Ronnie, to pair with the wines served by the invited winemaker. Set in a private room inside Tiki's, these almost immediately began selling out. The intimate vibe allowed winemakers to mingle with attendees, as well as for Ronnie to come out and describe why he selected each course, providing both education into flavor profiles as well as entertainment for his guests.

Recently, local brewing companies have hosted dinners with Chef Ronnie, yet again providing a bolstered experience for fans of Tiki's. Matching varied beer styles with hearty dishes like homemade gnocchi and rabbit ragout or lamb stew with porters, stouts and IPAs has excited both local attendees and the Tiki's kitchen staff as well.

During August of 2014, Bill Tobin sent Chef Ronnie to New York City with the coauthor of this book, Brian Berusch, to visit the restaurants and kitchens of more than 30 top eateries around Manhattan. The goal, to educate, taste and see where new experiences could be melded into the Tiki's atmosphere, resulted in meeting with personalities that included Daniel Boulud, Drew Nieporent, in addition to top talent at Momofuku, Mario Batali's Eataly and Po, Russ & Daughters, Gramercy Tavern, Blue Ribbon Bakery and more.

"It's been a blessing having Chef Ronnie work tirelessly in our kitchen," says Bill Tobin. "He's now part of the Tiki's family. He's elevated our former 'pub fare' to dishes that, in their own right, attract a cult following."

Grilled Hawaiian Akule Escabeche, White Anchovies, Grilled Radicchio, Puffed Quinoa

THIS IS a dish that has traveled around the world to anywhere the Spaniards have been. Escabeche typically features fish, but can also utilize chicken, rabbit or pork—so try each and see which resonates with your friends or family. Although Spanish culture isn't prominent in Hawaii, the melting pot of cultures and cuisine is. Escabeche is typically eaten cold, although it can also be served hot. Best yet, simply serve it over your favorite starch, such as brown rice, quinoa or fresh pasta.

Escabeche Vinaigrette

In a small saucepan cook the bell peppers, onions and garlic in olive oil on medium high heat until the garlic turns light brown. Remove from the heat and add all the remaining ingredients except the fish sauce, salt and pepper. Put back on the heat and bring to a simmer, allowing the alcohol to slowly cook off. Add a little fish sauce and cracked pepper and taste for the salt content. The fish sauce will give a mild anchovy flavor and salt probably won't be necessary. Remove from the burner.

Balsamic Paint

Simmer both ingredients in a shallow nonreactive pan until syrup-like. Paint four plates with the syrup with a pastry brush.

Puffed Quinoa

Heat a sauce pan or small wok to medium-high temperature, add the oil but don't smoke it. Add the quinoa and shake it to even the heat. When it pops, transfer it immediately to some paper towels as it will keep cooking and turn bitter.

Grilled Radicchio

Wash, dry and quarter the radicchio lettuce the long way through the core so the leaves stay intact. Be sure not to cut off the core first! Slather on Caesar salad dressing.

To finish the dish, reheat a grill on medium high for the radicchio and fish fillets. Grill the akule fillets and radicchio and transfer to four plates. Spoon the juicy vegetable vinaigrette mixture over the fish and some on the plate. Garnish with white anchovies, edible flowers and micro herbs, spread out the tomatoes. Spoon some of the puffed quinoa on top of the fish and on the plate.

Serve and enjoy. The dish is designed to eat cold, too. To do this, put the vegetable vinaigrette right over the cooked fish in a sealable container and marinate overnight. Then eat with greens cold!

Serves 4

Escabeche Vinaigrette

½ cup each red, yellow and green bell pepper, julienned

½ cup sweet onion, julienned

1 tablespoon rough cut fresh garlic

Extra virgin olive oil

2 tablespoons of capers with their juice

1 tablespoon each fresh chopped thyme, oregano and cilantro

½ teaspoon of toasted ground cumin

½ teaspoon ground coriander

½ teaspoon crushed red chilies (or chili pepper water, to taste)

1 cup of dry white wine

Juice of 1 lemon

4 tablespoons of rice wine vinegar

3 bay leaves

Fish sauce, to taste

Freshly cracked pepper, to taste

Balsamic Paint

½ cup dark balsamic vinegar

1 tablespoon white sugar

Puffed Quinoa

1 tablespoon vegetable oil

2 tablespoons red quinoa

Grilled Radicchio

One head radicchio

Caesar salad dressing as needed

Akule

2 each Hawaiian akule* (about a pound each), scaled, gutted and filleted

Sea salt, freshly cracked pepper and olive oil as needed

Anchovies, edible flowers, micro herbs, and halved island grape tomatoes for garnish

*Akule is in the scad or mackerel family. You can use something similar from our local fish market, or as Chef Ronnie mentions, replace with chicken, rabbit or pork as the Spanish do with variations of this dish.

Dear Mom,

Sometimes I think about how ridiculous it must seem to you and the family back in Nebraska; here I am, going about my days in a place with palm trees and warm turquoise waters all around. Whether I'm taking the kids to school, going for a jog or heading into Tiki's, I glimpse something anyone in Nebraska would think is a postcard of paradise. Even I think: ridiculous!

This ties to a story I wanted to share with you today. Last weekend Tracy and I headed over to Maui for the exquisite Kapalua Food & Wine Festival held at the Ritz-Carlton Kapalua. Talk about spoiled. And yet this was "research & development" for work. Naturally.

Throughout the four-day event, there are dine-around tastings that pair amazing seafood dishes with hundreds of wines poured in little tastes under various tents. Winemakers come from Napa and Sonoma, Washington and Oregon, Australia, New Zealand and elsewhere to introduce attendees to their wines.

During the day there are chef demonstrations, like something you might see on Emeril's show. A top chef might walk spectators through preparing a dish, sharing methods and instruction. There are "vertical" wine tastings, where you sample a flight of one type of wine from various makers to understand the nuances of a year, a region or a grape varietal. It's educational, yes, but it's incredibly fun.

One of the days we signed up for a special excursion that seemed harmless: A jeep ride into the West Maui Mountains to tour the fields where the famous Maui Gold pineapples are grown. From the mid-nineteenth through nearly the twentieth centuries, Hawaii was a leading exporter of pineapple. As labor and land became more expensive, places like the Philippines, Ecuador and other South American nations took over. But a few hundred acres on Maui remain spotted with amazingly sweet, low-acid pineapples. (Did you know it takes eighteen months for a single pineapple to grow from a plant? And that the window for it to be picked at its prime is only a few days?)

So we rode up to the Kapalua-owned pineapple farms, where a local chef was set to prepare an outdoor meal and serve us right there in the fields. At a thousand feet up the mountain, you're treated to vistas of Molokai and Lanai across wide expanses of blue. Gentle trade winds typically blow just enough to keep you cool, tousling your hair in the breeze.

Not this day.

When we arrived to the fields, red dust from the claylike ground was swirling. Bits of black plastic—laid underneath the soil to deter pests—were carried with the wind, sticking to our clothes and giving us the appearance of walking trash heaps. It was beautiful, but it was a wind tunnel.

Bev Gannon awaited us in a tiny tent she'd set up to ensure her burners wouldn't peter out while she cooked for us. As a restaurateur, I could see this might be a nightmare scenario for someone trying to put her best knife forward. To make it worse, most of the

guests were media invited from the mainland to experience one of Maui's top chefs, as well as sample dishes that featured Maui's best pineapple.

Yet Bev Gannon was steadfast, cool even. She's a Southerner, from Texas originally. Even after twenty-seven years operating one of Maui's longest-running restaurants, Hali'imaile General Store, she still has a warm, welcoming drawl. Bev had made a name for herself in Hawaii for delicious comfort food using island ingredients.

With a cocktail in one hand, Bev somehow managed to plate three courses for the twenty-five or so of us, and they were delicious. She individually seared plump chicken breasts with her special Southern crisped skin, topped with a pineapple relish that she taught us how to make. She ended the day by making sure that we, too, each had a cocktail (locally distilled vodka and pineapple juice with a dash of grenadine and house-made ginger syrup) and a delightful pineapple upside-down cake. Dessert was finished with ice cream Bev had made using goat's milk from a dairy a few miles from her restaurant.

It wasn't the most peaceful day on the mountain, but where a different, more tightly wound chef might have lost his cool, Bev Gannon was a portrait of grace. Plates were blowing over, flower garnishes went flying across tables from dishes to laps and blouses. It was pure comedy; we all had an hilarious if not unforgettable time.

I've since visited Hali'imaile General Store in Upcountry Maui and adored the experience there. Bev has since taken over a sprawling space at the Wailea Golf Course, where she feeds the golf and resort crowd, and she's expanding her reach. I think you'd love meeting her, Mom. I hope I can bring you to Maui on your next visit and see if we can have an experience worth writing home about.

With love, Bill

Bev Gannon

Bev Gannon is a Maui treasure. Before she became a celebrated chef and restaurateur, Bev road managed Liza Minnelli among other '70s acts. After a few years in show biz, she enrolled in London's Le Cordon Bleu and studied with Jacques Pepin himself. It was on the road cooking for touring rock stars that she met her husband, Joe Gannon, who'd been in the music business since the 1950s. It's said that her Southern roots and bold cooking can bring high-flying hard rockers back to earth with one plate of her down home food.

After relocating and launching a successful catering company on Maui, the Gannons bought the Hali'imaile General Store in 1987, formerly a dry goods shop for Upcountry pineapple and sugarcane plantation workers. As one of the original dozen Hawaii Regional Cuisine founders, Bev has been plating up generous helpings of what she calls "eclectic American" with Hawaiian flair, Asian influence and big, Southern overtones: the kind of food that makes you feel like a kid at your favorite auntie's house—the one that wants to spoil you and fatten you with heaping portions just to put a smile on both your faces.

Along the way Bev was selected by Hawaiian Airlines to be one of the first corporate rock star chefs to design in-flight meals, which earned her culinary accolades and even more national media attention.

Bev will candidly tell you that she opened her Upcountry "store" (as she calls the restaurant) long before it was cool to cook in rural paradise. She's been doing farm-to-table since the beginning, not so much to put herself on the vanguard but rather as a matter of practicality; the Maui farmers in Kula and Haiku, the ranchers in Makawao, are located just down the road and make great product. She feels pride in doing them justice by keeping things simple on the plate, and she still cooks with those same principles today.

Cashew Crusted Fresh Catch (Mahimahi) with Red Curry Coconut Sauce, Forbidden Rice

THIS IS a perennial favorite of the chef's because it's relatively simple, yet packs a strong, Asian-influenced punch that will really impress your dinner guests. In true Bev style it's a lovely, elegant presentation that rides the line between "comfort food" and high-concept.

Preheat the oven to 400°F.

In a small bowl, mix together the mayonnaise and sambal. Set aside.

In a food processor, pulse together the toasted panko and cashew nuts. Put in a medium bowl. Toss in the chopped cilantro, salt and pepper to taste. Set aside.

In a medium saucepan over medium heat, add the canola oil. Add the lemongrass and curry paste and sauté for 2 minutes. Add the pineapple juice to deglaze. Add the coconut milk and simmer for 10 minutes. Mix the cornstarch with water until there are no lumps. Add to the curry sauce. Simmer for another 4 minutes. Using an immersion blender, blend to a thick creamy consistency. Set aside.

To make the rice, in a strainer, rinse the rice under cold water for 2 to 3 minutes.

In a 5-x-7-inch casserole, add the rice and coconut milk, stir. Tightly cover with aluminum foil. Place in the preheated oven and bake for 20 minutes. Remove the foil and stir. Cover and put back into the oven for another 20 minutes. Uncover and fluff with a fork. Add the lime juice, butter and salt and pepper. Cover and keep warm.

Place the cashew crust mixture in a pie tin. Salt and pepper both sides of the fish. Brush one side of the fish with the sambal mixture to coat and then place that side down onto the crust mixture. Press the fish into the crust. Remove and place on a plate. Repeat for all pieces of fish.

In a large coated sauté pan on medium high heat, add the canola oil. When the oil is hot, place the fish crust side down into the pan. Cook for 2 minutes or until the crust is golden brown and then turn fish over. Turn the heat down to medium low and cook the fish another 5 to 6 minutes or until just cooked through.

To serve, place a scoop of rice in the center of the plate. Flatten the rice. Place the fish on the rice. Pour the sauce around the fish.

Serves 6

½ cup homemade or Best Foods mayonnaise
1 tablespoon sambal (Vietnamese chili paste)
½ cup panko, toasted to golden brown
½ cup dry roasted cashews, crushed
2 tablespoons cilantro, finely chopped
Salt and pepper
1 tablespoon canola oil
1 tablespoon lemongrass, finely minced, white part only
2 tablespoons red Thai curry paste
½ cup pineapple juice
3 cups coconut milk
2 tablespoons cornstarch
¼ cup water
2 cups forbidden rice
4 cups coconut milk
1 tablespoon lime juice
1 tablespoon butter
6 (5-ounce) pieces mahimahi (or flaky white fish)

Dear Mom,

As you might have guessed, I've been climbing the steep learning curve that comes along with a life in the restaurant industry. For someone who hasn't trained his whole life in food—to shift, for example, from engineering and construction to the food and retail business—running a restaurant is quite the departure. Yet, it certainly has its benefits.

One aspect that I find really astonishing is that someone can eat at home or dine in restaurants of all types and never think too deeply about what goes on the plate. But immerse yourself in this business and every component—even the plate itself—is weighed, discussed and tested. Then it's weighed again and criticized by customers. It's tweaked, restructured and reborn before finally reaching a menu. Whether it's a nouveau fast-food burger joint or a Michelin-rated fine-dining experience, the trials and tribulations differ in degree but not in kind.

The chef here in Hawaii who really opened my eyes to dinner plate composition is Colin Hazama. As a young chef with amazing chops and pedigree, he's incredibly refined. His meticulous platings come from training with some of the most storied chefs in America, including Jean-Georges Vongerichten.

I first sampled his wares at a restaurant called Hoku's, inside the Kahala Resort (where Tracy and I had our rehearsal dinner). Tucked away from bustling Waikiki, this Honolulu hotel is perched on its own private cove, with stunning, oasislike views and live dolphin swimming in a lagoon that skirts the pool. Chef Colin transformed a somewhat

staid and typical hotel eatery into a culinary experience. He took a unique approach and revisited dishes that leaned towards Middle Eastern and Mediterranean flavor profiles—two things we don't see much of in Hawaii—while also maintaining the hotel's famous curry bar. He was not only consistent, but he approached all his menu items with a sensitivity to the diverse clientele that gravitates to this classic location. A typical evening in the Hoku's dining room could see Hollywood actors, billionaire financial magnates and local residents. For a young chef who had recently returned to Hawaii from an intensive education on the mainland and was probably eager to put his new skills to test, he earned a reputation for pleasing everyone. He won a number of followers here, and I am among them.

Chef Colin did a few other stints on Oahu before getting "called up to the majors": When Jean-Georges Vongerichten hand-selected him to helm his first signature eatery in Hawaii, Colin accepted the challenge. As chef d' cuisine at the newly opened St. Regis Princeville on Kauai, a more gorgeous dining room could not be envisioned. Floor-to-ceiling glass walls give diners the sensation that they are hovering over the waters in Hanalei Bay. "Bali Hai" views face waterfalls and the lush interior of Kauai.

I was blessed to be invited to the one-year anniversary of Kauai Grill and flew over for the special dinner Colin orchestrated. From the minute I walked into the restaurant, I was transported. He curated an experience that was somehow simultaneously extravagant yet understated. The six-course meal (paired with wines) was a dizzying array of Kauai and neighbor island-harvested items. I "endured" a slow-cooked local abalone that floated in a chili-ginger broth. A poisson cru—Tahiti's version of ceviche—featured hirame, a fish Hazama snagged from the Natural Energy Lab on Hawaii Island (where they pump cold water from thousands of feet below the ocean's surface to holding tanks in order to harvest cold-water fish). He involved Kauai-grown watercress that was both peppery and luscious, which somehow brought together the coconut and yuzu flavors. Something I think you'll find interesting, Mom. Even though ceviche is technically "raw" fish, the citrus used in the dish (here it's yuzu, an Asian cross between a mandarin orange and a lemon) technically "cooks" the fish. Many cultures use this practice to make their raw fish preparations a little safer. Wild!

He turned up the volume with a cold mussel and Kekaha (local Kauai) shrimp that mingled on the plate with homemade chorizo, Kula onions and basil oil. Only this chef could take such eclectic flavors and meld them this delicately on the plate. I had a moi—a Hawaiian fish once reserved only for royalty—crusted in nuts and seeds that was so light, it seemed to float in the sweet and sour jus over which it was served. If this doesn't sound over the top already, Hazama nearly knocked me over with a Maine lobster tail served with a galangal and Champagne sabayon topped with crystallized kaffir lime. Yowza!

It isn't easy for me to describe how ingeniously he plated these dishes. As best I can describe it, Mom, when each dish was put in front of me, it felt like someone had delivered a custom painting. They were works of art! And then, to think, we're implored to grab a utensil and dismantle such a great work, which only adds another layer to his artistry.

Since that mind-blowing dinner in 2010, Colin has returned to Oahu to open and run some fine kitchens. Regardless of the establishment, his precision on the plate opened my eyes to a new level of sophistication in the dining room. Colin was walking, cooking proof that drive and the opportunity to study with world-class chefs can indeed make for a ground-breaking career; and he's still in his thirties!

With love, Bill

HONOLULU

Colin Hazama
or Executive ious Chef

Colin Hazama

At the time of this writing Colin Hazama is only thirty-four, yet he's worked in the kitchens of Gary Danko (San Francisco), Jean-Georges Vongerichten (New York & Kauai), Alan Wong (Honolulu) and Thomas Keller (San Francisco), among others. He's had a dream education in the culinary arts, trained by masters to lead their breakout kitchens and working alongside them at events. And he's not wasted what he's learned.

Colin started at Kapiolani Community College studying marketing, advertising and fine art before jumping to the California Culinary Academy in San Francisco. He transitioned to Roy Yamaguchi's Bay Area kitchen before moving on to Restaurant Gary Danko.

"I learned a lot from Alan Wong and Roy Yamaguchi," Colin says, "but Danko took it to the next level. That's where I honed my contemporary American techniques and refined my flavor profiles."

Colin returned to Hawaii to work at Hoku's in the Kahala Resort, where he stayed for three years before the opportunity arose to serve as the private chef for a wealthy family in Brazil. There Colin was able to experience more of the world, sample new ingredients and play with different course meals, ethnic cuisines and impromptu party foods.

He jumped to crafting tapas at Rumfire in the Sheraton Waikiki, a happy hour bar with a wall full of rum and a hipster clientele; then he became executive sous chef at Kauai Grill—Jean-Georges' first Hawaii eatery. To prepare, Colin spent time in each of Jean-Georges' New York City kitchens (there were seven at the time), learning the ins and outs of every dish on each restaurant's menu. He returned to Oahu in 2010 and became top chef at Sheraton Waikiki. He's recently moved to the Royal Hawaiian Hotel, the storied "Pink Palace of the Pacific."

Colin calls all the chefs with whom he's worked mentors, but it's Alan Wong that "taught me to look at the whole plate," he says. "He made me a really well-rounded chef."

Watching Colin plate a dish is like watching a painter at work. His fingers move across the plate in methodic sweeps. What's left is a masterwork, whether it's a fine-dining tasting menu or a banquet plate. Colin consistently pushes the limits of what can be done on a large scale, so it's no wonder he's found a niche directing culinary programs at large hotels.

Asian "Poisson Cru" with Bigeye Ahi & Kona Kampachi, Hydroponic Watercress, Coconut Yuzu

ALTHOUGH CHEF COLIN is one of the most technically proficient chefs in Hawaii—and his platings reflect his mastery of artful compositions—this sashimi dish is surprisingly easy to compose. Once again, by procuring the best fish attainable, you're guaranteed to wow diners around your table. Toss in a few edible flowers for some pops of color, and it's a meal everyone will remember for a long time.

Coconut Yuzu Cream

In a small saucepan, combine all the ingredients except for the yuzu juice and cornstarch. Bring to a boil and simmer for 10 minutes on low heat. Add a little water to the cornstarch to make the slurry. Whisk the cornstarch into liquid until sauce thickens, remove from heat, let sauce cool, add the yuzu juice and reserve.

Shichimi Oil

Combine all ingredients in a small saucepan over medium heat. Bring up to 185°F, take off the heat and remove. Let sit for 15 minutes and strain the oil through a fine-mesh sieve. Set aside.

"Poisson Cru"

Combine the cubed fish, coconut yuzu cream and poisson cru ingredients in a small bowl.

To serve, place 2 slices of ahi and 2 slices of Kampachi in alternating pattern on plate. Place a thin line of the cubed poisson cru on top of or next to sliced fish on the plate. Drizzle with the shichimi oil and garnish with breadfruit or taro chips and the watercress.

Serves 4

Fish

2 (8-ounce) blocks sashimi grade ahi tuna (half sliced and half cubed)

2 (8-ounce) blocks sashimi grade Kampachi* (half sliced and half cubed)

Coconut Yuzu Cream

1 cup coconut milk (Chaokoh brand)

¼ cup sugar

½ tablespoon kosher salt

1 ounce ginger, smashed

1 stalk lemongrass, smashed and bruised

2 tablespoons yuzu juice (or local lime juice)

½ tablespoon cornstarch

Shichimi Oil

2 tablespoons dry shichimi peppers

1 cup grape seed oil

½ tablespoon kosher salt

"Poisson Cru"

1 cup of the cubed ahi

1 cup of the cubed Kampachi

½ cup of coconut yuzu cream

¼ cup of green onions thinly sliced

¼ Maui onions or sweet onions, thinly sliced

½ Thai chili, minced

1 tablespoon of pickled ginger

2 kaffir lime leaf, minced

Salt and pepper to taste

Shichimi oil

16 breadfruit chips

½ cup hydroponic watercress (wash cleaned, stems removed)

*Kampachi falls into the Amberjack family. You could replace with yellowtail.

Dear Mom,

There's a story that I'm excited to share with you. It's a truly modern Hawaii story, and I feel blessed to have a connection to such things here in the islands.

Mark Noguchi is a friendly, gregarious and cheerful chef. The opposite of shy, he can light up a room with his infectious belly laugh. And he can really cook. He's also a spiritual person—something I wouldn't have guessed from casually interacting with him in social settings or at food events over the years. I learned about his background from his wife, Amanda, who does the marketing and event management for Pili Group, their joint effort catering and culinary company.

When he was younger, Mark was an avid hula dancer; he continued to dance through his early twenties. In Hawaii, studying hula doesn't mean you own a bunch of grass skirts

and like shaking your hips for laughs at the beach. A hula practitioner immerses him or herself to learn an ancient form of storytelling. Through chant, song and movement, hula tells a story of Hawaii—it's a discipline that people in Hawaii (and abroad) spend decades to master. It's a course of study as well as a lifestyle, and it has a large set of devotees who follow *kumu hula*, or learned elders who have mastered the art.

Mark studied with the legendary kumu hula Nalani Kanaka'ole on Hawaii Island. Nalani and her husband Sig Zane (a renowned fashion designer) run a *halau*, or hula school, near Hilo. It was there that Mark's passion for all things Hawaii deepened.

After full hula immersion in his early twenties, Mark attended the Culinary Institute of the Pacific. He went on to the Culinary Institute of America in Hyde Park, New York. While in school, as he learned various styles of cooking techniques and ingredients, Mark's hula practice started to become more salient in his mind. Even in New York's Hudson Valley in the winter time, he thought about Hawaiian culture and the ways in which foods like taro root were used over the centuries throughout Polynesia. He started thinking about cooking over open fires, steaming fish and meats in ti leaves, a practice older than Hawaiian culture. All this was dancing in his mind as he learned from the culinary leaders in the nation's HQ of food education.

When Mark returned to Oahu, he took those practices with him to various restaurants where he worked, often under the tutelage of great Hawaiian chefs. But it was his hula

studies so many years before, he says, that really influenced his ingredient pairings and preparations. It was all about keeping true.

Anyway, Mom, I give you all this background because the way I met Mark is ironic in light of it. Tracy's family had invited us to a catered party in Maunawili, a beautiful tropical neighborhood near Kailua, on the Windward side of Oahu. The caterer turned out to be Mark's Pili Group.

The food absolutely blew me away. He served a piece of pork that was so tender and supple, I had never tasted anything like it. When I spoke with him after dinner, he told me it had been prepared sous vide—vacuum sealed in a plastic bag and cooked slowly over low heat, typically in water. The style isn't much different from how pigs are cooked in an imu, a hole dug in the ground and lined with heated rocks. Pacific Island people have used such earth ovens since prehistoric times. The meat is wrapped in ti leaves, which keeps it tender by locking in moisture. The low temperature means that the collagens and proteins in the meat don't become tough and chewy. Sous vide has become a popular practice at smaller restaurants, where a chef can work some magic in an intimate setting and the payoff is big.

We had a wonderful experience with Mark and his team at that family meal. Mark works closely with many of his friends and family. He and Amanda have now started a family of their own; their kids will certainly be among the best fed children in the islands!

Mark has gotten a lot attention in recent years. He was on various national food shows for his Heeia Pier plate lunches, and he's since moved on to prepare the food at the Hawaiian Airlines employee cafe. He also runs the Mission Social House & Cafe, located inside the Mission Houses Museum in downtown Honolulu.

I believe Mark's "magic" emanates from his steadfast dedication to Hawaiian culture, and those values translate to the dinner plate. Mark takes a simple approach and then applies his education, training and experience. He then filters his concepts through what he's learned through hula: grace, clarity, precision and aesthetics. I love that he's melding this aspect of Hawaiian culture with what I call "the new Hawaiian Regional Cuisine."

I believe Mark's best days are yet to come. He's bounced around the islands' kitchens and has yet to truly root himself in an establishment. He could continue to cater and provide off-site services, as well as remain a presence at food events (he's prominent at the annual Hawaii Food & Wine Festival), but I think the dining scene would be a better place with more of Mark's food in it.

With love, Bill

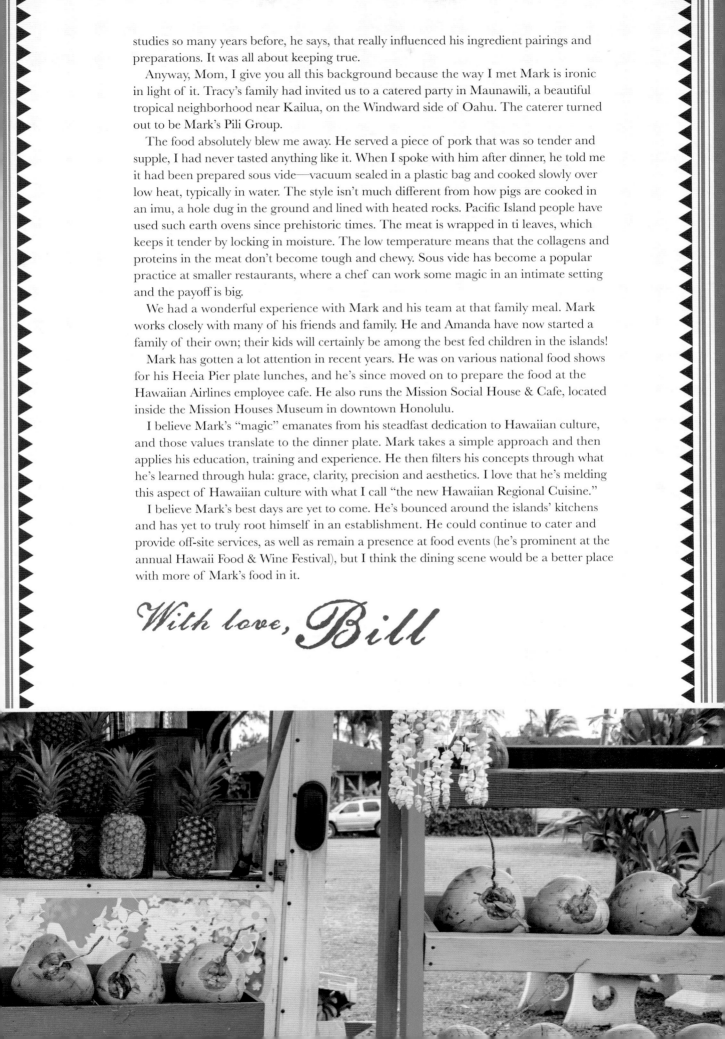

Mark Noguchi

Mark Noguchi is one of the more enigmatic chefs on Oahu. The first thing that comes to mind with Mark is that he's jovial. He has a warm, cherubic smile on his face nearly all the time. He's always producing a guttural laugh from his core. He's a blast to be around. Which is interesting when you consider that Mark's cooking comes from a very serious, spiritual place. Mark's equipped with a refined education at the Culinary Institute of the Pacific (Hawaii) and the Culinary Institute of America (Hyde Park, New York). He's got experience in various upscale kitchens across the mainland (L'Impero with Scott Conant; Rick Orlando at New World in Woodstock, New York; and with Peter Timmins at the Greenbrier in West Virginia). He's worked in some of Honolulu's finest restaurants, including Chef Mavro and Town, and he was co-owner and chef at Heeia Pier General Store & Deli. But for all this, his cooking comes from another place entirely.

Mark credits his passion for prep to his early twenties and the years he spent practicing hula with Halau o Kekuhi in Hilo. He danced and studied ancient Hawaiian practices under *kumu hula* (hula master) Nalani Kanaka'ole. For those not from Hawaii, the ancient style of hula, called *kahiko*, is very different from the modern form, called *auana*, that many presume is the whole of the art. Before the arrival of Europeans to Hawaii, ancient Hawaiians danced their genealogies and myths, performed hula to celebrate milestones (births, deaths) and to honor the *alii*, or chiefs. The art of *mele* hula requires considerable dedication—often decades of practice to achieve the slightest accomplishment—as well as rigorous physical training. Within the training, students learn the connections to the islands' environment, history and more.

Mark has, from the very beginning, been vocal about the fact that his passion for cooking stems from his hula practice.

"The way we make lei—picking foliage, treating the plant and forest with respect—it's the same way I treat ingredients and expect my chefs to," he says. "It's a privilege to say we call Hawaii home, that we were born and raised here. Those of us tapped to be a voice of Hawaii, it's a pretty awesome responsibility. I try very hard to be very conscious of that privilege. I don't take it for granted."

What I also really appreciate about Mark is his sense of place within a tradition. He is quick to acknowledge his culinary predecessors.

"What makes what we do successful is a testament to what Mavro, Wong and Roy did. They created this manifesto touting the best Hawaii had to offer, during a time when there wasn't a lot of great food for visitors. They stuck their necks out and it enabled us, the next generation, to do things like build a wood oven inside a bar and crank out authentic Neapolitan pizza with all local ingredients," he says. Mark also points to his contemporaries, chefs like Chris Kajioka and Andrew Le, as groundbreaking culinary leaders in Hawaii.

"Chris is one of the most technically proficient cooks in the nation," Mark says. "He has access to the finest ingredients in the world, but he still chooses local. And what Andrew is doing at the Pig and the Lady—progressive Vietnamese while melding in traditional Vietnamese. And stacking Hawaiian ingredients and killer cocktails. I mean, come on. We've made leaps."

Finally, I love that Mark is a dedicated family man. He's set up a business with his wife, Amanda, called Pili Group, that caters off-site and brands themselves in various locations. Their core principles are simple: community, education and food. It might be the Hawaiian Airlines employee kitchen, a museum cafe or a private dinner for a gala. But they sink all their aloha and mana into their dishes, hoping to empower their community through food education and then create a dialogue around the shared experienced. What better honor is there in food?

"I appreciate life and the learning I received on the mainland," Mark says. "But for me, you don't have to want something over the fence. It's about loving what you have in front of you. I don't have any negative feelings about anywhere. But I am a part of Hawaii."

Fried Catch, Farmers' Market Salad, Lechon Kawali Vinaigrette

HAVING MADE a name for himself as the locally sourced, sustainable and community-based chef around Oahu, it's no wonder that Chef Mark was so eager to share recipes that he gave us three to include. Mark's comfort zone is cooking for a few dozen friends, whether they are a hula halau, wedding party or kids. So this dish is approachable, delicious and easy to execute.

Combine all the fish fry ingredients, including the Mochiko rice flour and cornstarch.

Cut your fresh, locally sourced fish (salmon, mahimahi, scallop, shrimp or whatever is procured closest to your home) into 2-x-3-inch pieces. Toss in the fish fry flour mixture and reserve off to the side. (You can do this a few hours ahead of time if you like.)

Heat a pot or wok of oil to 375°F. Have a spider skimmer, a pair of tongs, and a paper towel–lined cake pan ready, as well as the reserved seasoning.

Working in small batches, fry the fish until crisp and golden brown. Immediately transfer to the prepared pan and season.

To make the salad, soak the onions in ice water for 30 minutes. In the meantime, drop the long beans in boiling water for 20 to 30 seconds, and then shock them in ice water, drain and reserve. In a stainless steel bowl, combine all the salad ingredients.

To make the vinaigrette, place all the ingredients in a small bowl and whisk to combine. Dress the salad with the vinaigrette. Taste and adjust with more salt and pepper as you like.

Arrange the fish on a plate and top with the dressed salad.

Serve with rice and cold beer.

Serves 4

Fish Fry

½ cup garlic salt

½ cup pepper

½ cup kosher

½ teaspoon cayenne

1½ cups Mochiko (rice flour)

1½ cups cornstarch

2 pounds local fresh fish

Farmers' Market Salad

1 red onion, sliced paper thin

1 pound Hōʻio long bean or green bean, cleaned and sliced on a 2-inch bias

3–4 stalks green onion (scallion), sliced paper thin

1 pound heirloom or local tomato, diced

1 Japanese cucumber, deseeded and sliced

1 Hawaiian or Thai bird chili, finely minced

3 cloves garlic, microplaned or finely minced

¼ cup dried shrimp or cuttlefish, chopped

Arugula, optional

Lechon Vinaigrette

14 cloves Garlic

1 cup Olive Oil

3 pieces Limes, juiced

3 tablespoons apple cider vinegar

1 tablespoon white vinegar

1 tablespoon Shoyu

½ tablespoon Patis

All roasted garlic purée

½ cup roasted garlic oil

4 tablespoons pepper

Salt to taste

Dear Mom,

Have you heard about this new trend of food trucks that are a mash-up of different cuisines? There's a Korean-inspired taco truck in Los Angeles. One that serves ramen burgers in San Francisco. New York has single-sourced coffee and organic, hand-crafted ice cream trucks. Is there anything like this back in Nebraska? What about the "pop up" movement? Where chefs forgo the concept of finding a restaurant location and, instead, set up one-night or weeklong "pop up" service in an empty warehouse, or in a field, or an art gallery? Ever heard of such a thing?

At first I thought it was crazy. Perhaps a sign of young millennial chefs with deep-seeded commitment issues. But then it dawned on me . . . in the current age of disruptive technology, direct-to-consumer products, news-by-social-media and the removal of "the middle man," why not lose the anchor of an unsurmountable rent and overhead if you can pull off a few nights of magic and move on? Admittedly, it's not for everyone. But it's now a social movement that has a following all over the United States. And in my guestimation, it will result in a shift in the way people dine across America.

One chef in particular here in Hawaii is leading that charge. His name is Andrew Le, and he comes from a fascinating background, like so many here. His parents are Vietnamese, both were born and raised there, each escaping the Vietnam War and migrating to Hawaii. What they took with them and instilled in their children was a love for Vietnamese cooking. It remained as their sole tie to the land of their heritage—something they shared with many immigrants to Hawaii in the twentieth century.

Andrew dug into a life of cooking, working with Chef Mavro and learning quite a bit from Mavro's sous chef, Kevin Chong. Yet, spending his evenings in Chinatown as the

arts, music and young cultural developments were exploding there in the early 2000s, Andrew was getting antsy to make his mark.

He started doing pop-up dinners in restaurants that were only open for lunch, working out a deal with the owners. They started as no more than twenty-five people, music playing from a radio on the floor, and nothing but a table and disposable place settings. They very quickly grew to 3-day events with people vying for tickets. And not unsurprisingly, Andrew was serving an evolution of what he grew up eating. He was plating a blend of traditional Vietnamese fare—pho, noodle dishes, pork and more—melded with fresh Hawaiian ingredients and some new techniques learned in the Mavro kitchen. Whatever he was doing was striking a major chord with young diners.

The demand was so high, he eventually began setting up regular pop ups at farmers' markets and in a food truck. Thanks to a quickly developing social media following, he started making a name for himself as the leader of pop up food events.

Andrew struck gold with a lease in a brick-lined restaurant on King Street in Chinatown. Tracy and I started going directly after it opened, and it never disappoints. Andrew has crafted a very communal, bright and energetic dining room in Pig and the Lady that feels like a big party. People sit at long tables end-to-end with other diners, allowing you to see what others are ordering. There's a wonderfully creative cocktail menu. And I hear Andrew's mom is often back in the kitchen testing and honing his pho broth!

He's built up not only a proven following, but his staff has become an extended family, he says—and you can sense it when you're seated in the dining room, observing the waitstaff and chatting with table mates. And the dishes . . . he's using everything he can source locally and plating consistently innovative dishes that are rooted in Vietnamese flavor profiles. Such a unique offering!

The manner in which new food trends are taking root here in Honolulu is amazing, Mom. There are ties to nearly every corner of the globe. What a privilege to be here, in this relatively small place smack dab in the Pacific Ocean and watch it unfolding. What a ride!

With love, Bill

Andrew Le

Andrew Le earned his stripes working under the tutelage of Chef Mavro, who at the time, employed chef Kevin Chong in the same kitchen. One of the finest testing grounds for culinary experimentation, Le's five years at Mavro gave him both the skills and confidence he needed to launch his own venture.

Andrew led the "pop up" charge during the onset of that culinary trend (2011) in Honolulu with a few special dinners at nondescript locations. He essentially incited a riot of ravenous followers who demanded consistency, prompting Andrew to set up weeks or monthlong service at other people's eateries, farmers' market stalls or in food trucks—wherever he could carve out enough space without actually acquiring his own.

All that changed in 2013 when he began setting up shop in a Chinatown location. Passing by his new front door was a steady stream of foot traffic: art enthusiasts, nightclub goers and anyone else heading out on the town in Honolulu's explosive arts district. Before he was able to open his doors, Le was named "Rising Star Chef, Hawaii" by StarChefs and also earned a nomination for a James Beard award ("Best Chef, West"). A fortuitous time to open a new restaurant, indeed.

Andrew's Pig and the Lady's brick-and-mortar location broke a few other Honolulu dining scene rules: long, communal tables allowed for guests to rub elbows with new people. Much attention was paid to the craft spirits and cocktail side of the menu. Names of drinks like "The Pig Lebowski" (a white Russian-style cocktail made with tequila and horchata) and "Sun King" (pisco, pineapple, egg froth and cardamom) were a great indicator of the starting point from which Le leapt into his approach to the accompanying food.

Le, all along, has plated variations on his upbringing in a Vietnamese household positioned in the middle of the Pacific Ocean. At times, his pop-ups or farmers' market offerings were straight traditional pho. Yet at Pig and the Lady, he was ready to cut loose and make a statement. Here, he melded contemporary executions he had learned between schooling (at the CIA in New York) and Chef Mavro's kitchen. His friends and supporters (Chris Kajioka and Mark Noguchi are two) tell people it's "a mash-up of traditional Vietnamese and modern Asian." But from our many meals here, we'd postulate that Le is doing a whole lot more.

He's spent considerable time in San Francisco absorbing the multicultural offerings in that city, and takes that sensibility into his Chinatown, Oahu, kitchen. What comes out can look like plates of hearty BBQ, or it can reflect the portioned out, multiflavor explosions of Vietnamese. He can serve a bowl of pho unparalleled in Honolulu, then elevate it by topping with a quail egg and sous vide pork belly if the mood strikes him.

Now entrenching, if not anchoring, Chinatown's foodie movement—which follows on the heels of a decade of arts happenings-cum-boutique clothing shops and restaurants—Le serves as de facto mayor of King Street.

Cha Ca La Vong

CHEF ANDREW'S mash-up of new and old Vietnamese dishes use fresh produce in tried-and-true preparations. This dish requires a bit of foresight: It's important to make the mam tom sauce (mam tom bac is fermented shrimp paste) ahead of time for it to properly develop; and your fish should marinate for at least 4 hours (if not a full day) in order to absorb the essence of his sumptuous marinade. In Andrew's words, "The mam tom sauce should be made 1 to 2 days in advance to allow for the flavors to develop and the funk of the shrimp paste to mellow."

To make the sauce, blend the pineapple, garlic, ginger, mam tom bac, sugar, lime juice, fish sauce and coconut water until smooth. Add the sambal and continue to blend, then store in the refrigerator.

For the fish marinade, clean and ready your blender again: put all the ingredients in and blend until smooth. You can marinate your fish the day before, or for a few hours.

Take your vermicelli noodles and follow the cooking instructions on the package. Drain, rinse and cool.

Mix all the herb ingredients together, reserve.

Remove your fish from the marinade and remove excess liquid. Over medium heat, coat a sauté pan with enough grape seed oil to cover the bottom. Once hot, carefully place the fish in the pan and cook for 3 to 4 minutes on each side, until golden brown. Take out of the pan and reserve.

To plate, arrange the vermicelli noodles in a bowl. Place the cooked catfish on top, sprinkle a spoonful each of fried shallots and roasted peanuts over the fish. Spread a generous amount of the herb mix on top and serve with the mam tom sauce on the side.

Serves 8

Mam Tom Sauce

225 grams pineapple

32 grams garlic, peeled and chopped

125 grams ginger, peeled and chopped

98 grams mam tom bac

280 grams sugar

380 grams lime juice

215 grams fish sauce

1 can of coconut water

125 grams chili sambal olek

Fish Marinade

100 grams shallot

300 grams galangal, peeled and chopped

160 grams fresh turmeric, washed well and chopped

150 grams ginger, peeled and chopped

25 grams dry turmeric

325 grams olive oil

900 grams plain yogurt

150 grams fish sauce

25 grams mushroom powder

60 grams sugar

Black pepper corns to taste

1 package of vermicelli noodles

Herb Mix

2 cups dill, cleaned and picked

2 cups mint, cleaned and picked

2 cups shiso, cleaned and picked

2 cups rau ram, cleaned and picked

2 cups onion sprouts, cleaned and picked

8 (10-ounce) fresh catfish fillets, skinned

Grape see oil for cooking

1 cup fried shallots

1 cup roasted peanuts, chopped

Dear Mom,

There's a local word for an indescribable feeling: Stoke. From what I can tell, it spun out of the surf community—that's where you'll hear it said most often. It refers to the feeling of elation you get when you're able to pull off something far beyond you, that's bigger than you, like surfing a wave. Stoke is part warm fuzzy feeling, part adrenaline rush and part deep appreciation. When a surfer rides a challenging wave with grace, they say they're "stoked."

But stoke doesn't stop at surfing. It can be applied to anything.

Chef Brian Etheredge on Maui exudes stoke. He hails from another warm-weather climate (Florida), and so he's assimilated to the islands well. He's put down roots with a young family and a thriving restaurant.

Brian picked an interesting location—a sleepy mountainside locale in Wailea, the resort area that features a Four Seasons, a Fairmont, an Andaz and others on a gorgeous swath of shoreline. The Hotel Wailea, where Brian has his restaurant, is a mile up a mountain road. The design of hotel's main building is a throwback to the 1960s, with a vast koi pond and two-story stone atrium in the lobby. When Brian decided to plant his flag here, the hotel was in flux, a struggling business with less-than-chic accommodations. A decade later, it's got wonderful owners and a savvy management team. After a yearlong renovation, Hotel Wailea now attracts a young jet-set and celebrity clientele looking to get away from the populous and often paparazzi-lined beaches of Wailea. All this bodes well for Brian and his unique Capische? restaurant.

I'm guessing, but the space he took over was probably once a Benihana-style teppanyaki joint with two oversized tabletop grills and a spacious garden area for seating. Rather than take the grills out, Brian came up with the "Il Teatro" concept: He consults with the booking party to gauge their interest level in certain foods. Then he crafts a menu of anywhere from five to twenty courses that cover the flavor profiles of a given region in Italy, a place he "goes to every single day, in my head," he says. Brian's team pairs wines with the dishes; occasionally they flip the script and courses are made to fit a wine that his sommelier or the guest wants to feature.

Il Teatro dinners have a cult following. Couples book them months in advance, celebrities and well-researched travelers set them up from offices in Los Angeles long before they head out for their Hawaii holiday. All the while Brian crafts impeccable dishes drawn from a complete dinner menu available to regular restaurant diners.

I first experienced Brian's food at the Taste of Wailea, one of the most spectacular food events in Hawaii. During June's Maui Film Festival, the organizers set up an array of food, spirit and wine booths on a hillside at the Wailea Golf Course overlooking the ocean. There's usually a band. People dress up. And since it's in the midst of the film festival, all of Maui clamors for tickets so they can rub elbows with celebrities and the Hollywood elite. For Maui's top chefs, it's a chance to put their best dishes forward, hoping to tempt new customers to their dining rooms later that week. But for attendees sipping fine cocktails at sunset while sampling the best from Maui's best chefs . . . it's unbeatable.

Tracy and I divided and conquered, each of us grabbing dishes served on compostable bamboo mini-plates and reconvening at a table to dig in. Brian's dish stood out first for presentation; I honestly had no idea what it was, but it was gorgeous. On first glance, I thought it was finely sliced ahi tuna, a staple on menus throughout Hawaii. Yet, something told me there was more. I took a bite, and my mouth filled with a completely unexpected sensation. I've said it before in these letters: Many of my biggest evolutionary food leaps have come from having my expectations blown apart. This was one of those times.

Once we finished, Tracy and I rose silently and headed over to talk to the chef. We had questions!

After a laugh, Brian told us the dish was called Vegan Sashimi. The bright red "tuna" was in fact watermelon! To make it, Brian compresses the watermelon in a vacuum sealer, then slices it thinly. He was excited to tell us that the process results in some concentrated bits of watermelon juice that look like veins, further fooling people into thinking it's fish. He tops the melon with wasabi and mint foam, then finishes the dish with a frozen radish sorbet.

It sounds wacky. Believe me, if I'd seen it on paper I would have been confused, too. But picture being outside during a glorious Maui sunset. It's hot, you're dressed for mingling with movie stars and Maui elite, and then this dish just knocks you off your feet. It's refreshing and bold, imploring you to seek more from its creator.

Tracy and I make a point to book a dinner at Capische? every time we go to Maui. Brian's rich, Italy-inspired dishes often feature fresh venison, bold sauces, rich choices in produce (like squash) and other surprises. I look forward to taking you there on your next visit.

With love, Bill

Brian Etheredge

Maui chef Brian Etheredge might be one of the most colorful and independent-minded culinary talents in Hawaii. He mans the helm of Capische? restaurant at Wailea—a hidden, tucked-in-the-hillside gem frequented by West Maui locals and *akamai* (clued-in) foodie travelers. As one of the co-owners, Brian not only brings his culinary and business acumen to the table but also a passion for the ingredients he uses.

Brian knew he wanted to cook when he was a thirteen-year-old kid growing up in Ponte Vedra Beach, Florida. He went on to train at New York's Culinary Institute of America with a focus in wine studies, and much of his food has wine in mind. He made a name for himself in a unique way: using a pair of teppanyaki grills—the kind you sit around at a Benihana restaurant—he crafted food that transported diners to the various regions of Italy. Brian never repeats the same menu twice, and he sources a mind-boggling array of local ingredients, including the under-appreciated venison from Molokai and Maui. A self-described aficionado of all things Italy, Brian modeled the menu at Capische? with the Slow Food movement in mind.

"The custom dinners we have done at the restaurant are not just an opportunity for our customers to try different regional cuisines, but they're a chance for our chefs to expand their knowledge of the regions of Italy. It keeps us engaged, which is the most important thing for a chef. It's easy for cooking to become rote—and this keeps us reading, scanning the Web for new things," says Brian. His Il Teatro menus can have anywhere from five to twenty courses. That keeps things interesting, and not just for his chefs. "Our regulars are our toughest customers," Brian grins. "They really push us to show them something they didn't see the last time they dined with us. So we're constantly scouring the nooks and crannies of Maui for new ingredients, as well as techniques. We'll incorporate molecular gastronomy when it's called for."

One example: Brian's version of bistecca fiorentina starts with a sous vide (slow cooked in a vacuum-sealed bag) Kobe beef tenderloin or ribeye. He'll serve it with rosemary potatoes, puréed arugula and mini gnocchi that are seared crispy tableside. The chef finishes the dish with a fried garlic gremolata atop the meat and potatoes.

In another dish, Brian reinvents an island favorite, the loco moco—typically a hamburger patty served over rice with a fried egg and brown gravy. His version uses braised oxtail atop a kabocha pumpkin and uni (sea urchin) risotto, finished with a sous vide quail egg. "I love that one," he says. "It shows the diner a bit from the north of Italy by using heavy flavors like the squash risotto and quail, with a bit of the sea from the south in the uni. In composition, this dish is all Hawaii."

As with many of the chefs featured in these pages, Brian is a family man. He's a new dad, in fact. On his downtime, you'll find him teaching his sons to spearfish in the warm West Maui waters or bow-hunting axis deer in the predawn hours—prior to a fifteen-hour day in the kitchen.

Snapper with Homemade Squash Tortellini

THIS FUN, Northern Italian–inspired dish allows for a piece of fresh fish to be accompanied by homemade, rich tortellini and a refreshing salad—it's the perfect fall or early winter fare. You'll need to practice up on your pasta-making skills, although the tortellini don't need to be masterpieces for this dish to shine. You can also get creative with the presentation, as Chef Brian did, serving this one on a black slate slab.

In a hot, lightly oiled pan, add the butter, sage, and the seasoned (salt and pepper) fish. Baste the fish with the butter and oil, leaving on skin side for most of the cooking. Remove when cooked to desired doneness.

Celeriac Purée
Boil the celery root until tender and place in blender. Add the cream and butter until desired consistency and flavor. Add 1 ounce at a time so you don't over do it. Add salt and pepper to taste.

Butter
Brown the butter in a hot pan, adding the squash, chestnuts and shallot. Cook until tender, then deglaze with sherry and bourbon.

Tortellini
Bake the squash (or use the leftover squash from the butter), put in a food mill with the cinnamon, nutmeg and salt and pepper.

Roll out the pasta dough and place 1 ounce of filling in dollops. Fold the tortellini (you can watch an instructional video online if need be, as it's fairly simple) and use egg wash to seal. Blanch when ready in boiling water, toss with the butter sauce.

Garnish the dish with parsley and frisée seasoned with the lemon juice.

Serves 4

Snapper
4 tablespoons olive oil
4 tablespoons butter
2 sprigs sage
2 (7-ounce) skin-on snapper, scales removed
Salt and pepper

Celeriac Purée
1 medium celery root, peeled and cubed
¼ cup cream
2 tablespoons butter
Salt and pepper to taste

Butter
8 tablespoons butter
1⅔ cups squash*, par baked in the oven (cook until just cooked)
4 chestnuts, crushed
1 whole shallot, sliced
Touch of sherry vinegar
½ cup bourbon of your choice

Tortellini
1 cup of cooked squash
Pinch of cinnamon
Pinch of nutmeg
Salt and pepper to taste
Pasta dough from recipe of your choice
Egg wash

Fresh parsley
Frisée
Lemon juice

*Chef Brian typically uses a Kabocha, but you can use seasonally available squash of your choice.

Dear Mom,

I was recently telling someone the anecdote about you getting kicked out of home economics class for making fun of the teacher. It dawned on me that you never considered yourself a "good" cook. All of my siblings would agree that we saw our share of mac 'n' cheese on the dinner table; but they'd also recall your roast beef and potatoes, or a slow-cooked pot roast with carrots. It would stew all day, wafting delightful scents throughout the house until we devoured it. Nothing can replace those memories or lessen the impact of that food.

I was thinking about how things started to evolve in both the food world and my appreciation for food. When you were putting yourself through nursing school in Omaha, you "found" restaurants between home and school (or work) and would occasionally bring us to them. That's where we had "Mexican" food, which consisted of hard yellow taco shells and ground beef with seasoning; or "Chinese" LaChoy poured over undercooked noodles. Looking back, those were shoddy attempts at ethnic cuisine. But to us—at a time when a trip to McDonald's was a big deal—it was out of the box. (And literally, too: they came out of a box.)

As a nation, we experienced the advent of new communication technology that gave us access to everything, everywhere, all the time. The Food Network brought the how-tos of every type of cooking to our living rooms. It seemed like just prior to that my entire world was the food you could find within a forty-mile radius of Omaha.

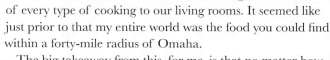

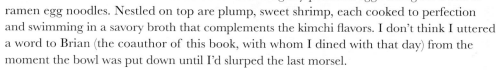

The big takeaway from this, for me, is that no matter how much you evolve, you will always feel a strong connection to your early food memories. Nothing lessens them. We all have our chicken noodle soup: nourishing, delicious and soul-filling.

The men who opened Lucky Belly in Honolulu's Chinatown take that idea to another level, or at least, put a cultural twist on it. Dusty Grable, a co-owner, turned a small corner bar into a minimalist eatery that churns out Hawaii's version of comfort food: steaming bowls of ramen and soft pork bao buns. As it turns out, that's comfort food for a lot of people. Their Korean-inspired kimchi bowl is ethereal. It arrives in a hearty ceramic vessel with a lightly poached egg resting on a bed of ramen egg noodles. Nestled on top are plump, sweet shrimp, each cooked to perfection and swimming in a savory broth that complements the kimchi flavors. I don't think I uttered a word to Brian (the coauthor of this book, with whom I dined with that day) from the moment the bowl was put down until I'd slurped the last morsel.

This is Honolulu's chicken soup.

Directly across the street, Dusty reimagined a SoHo, New York–style restaurant and fit it into another corner space that has become a popular eatery. Livestock Tavern is a design-forward, somewhat minimalist space with eclectic furnishings, a super-cool bar and a seasonal menu that's seemingly out of another urban landscape. During a fall dinner there I've had oysters Rockefeller, warmed brie with cranberry, apple and walnuts, as well as grilled brussels sprouts. To dine on Livestock's lobster and squid ink pasta, osso buco and pumpkin bread pudding in a cool setting is a unique experience in Hawaii.

This isn't typical Hawaii cuisine, yet to me it says that Grable and his chefs are eager to remind people that seasons dictate what's eaten elsewhere in the world (unlike here, where it's essentially a perpetual summer). For those who didn't grow up here, these are the foods that bring us back to times when we dined with loved ones on food that warmed more than our bellies. There's something deeply gratifying about eating a dish that connects you with another time and place, and I feel like both Lucky Belly and Livestock hit those receptors for people whether or not they are aware of it.

I know these places would remind you of nights out when the menus seemed like a foreign language, but we'd relish in both the flavors and making new memories.

With love, Bill

Dusty Grable

Dusty Grable might have been born and raised in Hawaii, but it took a two-year stint in San Francisco to kick his game up a notch before returning home to find his burgeoning Chinatown food empire. He opened his first restaurant, Lucky Belly, in 2012, taking a page from Momofuku's approach to simple ramen—that is, served with linen napkins and backed by a full bar. He tapped a former coworker and chef, Jesse Cruz, to partner with him on the venture. (The pair worked together at Formaggio in Kailua prior to Grable's move to the Bay Area.)

Situated on a high-traffic corner in bustling, revitalized Chinatown, where art galleries, boutiques and coffee shops are au courant, Lucky Belly is the spot with lines out the door for lunch and dinner. The Belly Bowls are as satisfying as they sound, with pork belly, smoked bacon and sausage in a rich broth. For those who want to take their ramen fixation to the next level, Lucky Belly is a must. In fact, our executive chef Ronnie Nasuti and writer Brian Berusch returned from a research trip in New York City to proclaim they both preferred Lucky Belly's noodle bowls to Momofuku's!

After a successful eighteen months, they secured another storefront catty-corner to Lucky Belly. Livestock Tavern has a spacious barroom and unique cocktail program—perhaps a nod to Grable's years working behind the bar at Restaurant Gary Danko and at the Ritz-Carlton in San Francisco, where he honed his business and people skills. Livestock's dining room hews to the minimalist farmhouse modern style that's sweeping hip neighborhoods nationwide. Yet at Livestock, Grable and Cruz are presenting their take on Hawaii Regional Cuisine at a high level.

Sourcing from around the globe while still spotlighting local ingredients, you might find duck liver profiteroles with fig jam on the same table as uni pasta or crisped snapper with "Manhattan stew."

Grable's approach echoes that of many other young chef-restaurateurs featured in these pages: Finding ways to combine the best of Hawaii's ingredients with well-researched platings from around the globe. This seems to be the face of Hawaii's avant cuisine.

Lucky Belly's Kimchi Bowl

THE LUCKY BELLY culinary team intentionally leaves the pork broth (base) completely open to you, the home chef, in order to adjust the flavors to your preferences. While the standard for pork broth is roasting then boiling pork knuckle (and other) bones for 12 to 24 hours with the addition of mirepoix (carrot, onion, celery), you can add or subtract additional root vegetables and even varied protein (like chicken or beef bones) to richen up the base of this dish. Whether you're slurping noodles after a long day of surfing or on a frosty winter day, this is a soul-pleasing dish that will be admired by many.

In a large pot, bring your favorite pork stock to a hard boil. Boil for 5 minutes.

Reduce to medium heat and add miso, sesame paste, dashi, konbu, and togarashi. Simmer for 25 minutes allowing the flavors to infuse.

Then, strain the broth through a fine-mesh strainer. If spiciness is preferred, white pepper is recommended.

Place the noodles in boiling water for exactly 3 minutes. Strain and add to the broth.

Add toppings as desired, such as kimchi, soft-boiled egg, shrimp, green onion, ginger or whatever suits your taste.

Serves 6

2 quarts pork stock

1 cup white miso

1 cup sesame paste

1 ounce hondashi (fish stock)

1 sheet konbu

1 tablespoon togarashi

White pepper, if desired

4 (5-ounce) ramen noodle portions

Ramen Toppings

2 ounces kimchi

1 soft-boiled 6-minute egg

3 togarashi spiced shrimp

1 ounce green onions, sliced

1 teaspoon ginger, minced

3 ounces bean sprouts, cooked

3 ounces wakame, hydrated

1 teaspoon roasted sesame seeds

2 tablespoons togarashi

Livestock Tavern's Winter Lamb Stew

READERS MAY be surprised to learn that seemingly wintry dishes have a home on the Hawaii dining table. The communal nature found in friends sharing a pot of stewed meat jibes with the celebration of eating Hawaiians love. Here, the culinary team at Livestock Tavern in Oahu's Chinatown presents a simple, hearty lamb stew. The use of cloves is what makes this dish otherworldly.

In a large rondeaux, sear the lamb till caramel brown in color. Reduce to medium heat. Add the vegetables, garlic and olive oil. Bring it to a simmer and add the roux to thicken, stirring occasionally. Pour in the lamb stock, red wine, tomato paste and herbs. Simmer until the vegetables and lamb are cooked through and tender.

Serves 6 to 8

4 pounds lamb shoulder, largely diced

4 carrots, largely diced

1 celery bunch, largely diced

2 leek stalks, diced

2 fennel bulbs, diced

8 whole garlic cloves

½ cup olive oil

1½ pound roux

2 quarts lamb or chicken stock

8 ounces tomato paste

1 cup red wine

1 tablespoon rosemary

1 tablespoon thyme

1 tablespoon parsley

1 bay leaf

Livestock Tavern Summer Cocktail: "Squints"
as created by Allie Haines

THE COCKTAIL program at Livestock Tavern may seem whimsical, but co-owner Dusty Grable's experience behind bars on the mainland shaped this well-regarded watering hole. Here, this somewhat tropical libation packs a flavorful punch—yet keeps things classy.

1½ ounces Kohana
¾ ounce lemon juice
½ ounce orange Curacao
½ ounce Orgeat
¼ ounce Luxardo
Barspoon of absinthe
Amaro Montenegro float
Mint leaves, for garnish

Combine all ingredients except for the Amaro Montenegro. Shake and double strain into a double rocks glass over crushed ice. Float the Amaro Montenegro and garnish with mint leaves.

Lucky Belly Cocktail: "Beanto Box"
as created by Christopher Nassar

PAIRING COCKTAILS with rich and hearty bowls of ramen isn't an easy task. The comprehensive whiskey menu at Lucky Belly makes for building blocks of equally satisfying happiness. This is a must for any whiskey enthusiast.

2 ounces Akashi whiskey
½ ounce Suze
½ ounce vanilla simple syrup
2 dashes Angostura bitters
Orange peel, for garnish

Add all ingredients into mixing glass. Stir and strain into a double rocks glass over one large ice cube. Garnish with the orange peel.

Dear Mom,

There's a chef in town named Ed Kenney, and with the sheer amount of press coverage he receives around here, I wouldn't be surprised if you've heard of him all the way in Nebraska. He's got sleeves of tattoos down his arms, hails from a prominent, well-connected Honolulu family and has really climbed his way through the culinary ranks in Honolulu. At a time when there was virtually no great Italian-style trattorias on the island, Ed opened Town restaurant in the sleepy Kaimuki suburb, just a few miles from Waikiki. The bare floors and walls, metal tables, recycled placemats and coasters, sustainable everything (he famously was one of the first restaurateurs around here to put a compostable worm tub behind his restaurant) really resonated with young folk eager for a taste of similar eateries in places like Brooklyn, New York, or San Francisco's Mission District. Ed struck gold and earned a steady following.

But it came on the heels of some experiments, as most successful business folk experience, not all big winners. Ed helmed Cafe Monserrat for a short time, where he had some winning dishes, but overall the concept wasn't accepted by locals nor tourists. Yet I find it's the best chefs or restaurateurs (or any business person, for that matter) that learns from their experiences and evolves from them who tend to shine brightest in the end.

For a time, Ed had a lunch outpost inside the Honolulu State Art Museum called "Downtown." I would pop in for great charcuterie sandwiches on hearty bread to-go, and relished in the side dishes you could select with each entrée. These often featured fascinating mash-ups of locally sourced ingredients, like kale or watercress

with fava beans, or faro pasta with local goat cheese, or something else entirely. It was in those small side salads that I tasted some unique flavor pairings I never would have experienced otherwise.

As Town continues to impress locals and in-the-know visitors, Ed has "doubled down" on his winnings and bought a building across Waialae Avenue from Town and opened Kaimuki Superette, a place where you can pick up sandwiches, fresh veggies or local offerings like musubi. Shortly thereafter, he opened Mud Hen Water, a bistro on the same stretch of avenue, with in and outdoor seating, where Ed cooks "Food reminiscent of my childhood." One thing is clear: Ed had a very unique, interesting childhood!

I spoke with Ed, and listened to how his mind journeyed from a nostalgic memory, to a menu item at Mud Hen Water; it was fascinating! He told me that one of his best memories was spending Sundays at a quirky Honolulu restaurant called The Willows, which is set in a tropical garden, smack dab in the middle of the city. Once inside, you wouldn't know you were in a bustling neighborhood. Koi ponds, big banyan trees, and tables meandering around the garden made it the perfect place for kids to run wild while the adults partook in their buffet.

Ed told me that he relished in this family time, much as I do. And one of the memories tied to that experience, for him, was the chicken curry buffet. He told me the bright yellow color—a melding of Japanese and Indian or Thai style curries that he says are unique to Hawaii—had a particular flavor. After plating, you could pick all the toppings you liked, including toasted coconut, bacon, sieved egg, green onion, peanuts and more. And this was accompanied by a baked banana.

When he was honing his chops in the kitchen—and reminiscing on this meal—he researched the history of bananas in Hawaii, which is long and storied. Ed is one of those chefs who loves a story behind a dish: And the Mai'a Maoli baked banana from Molokai was born. Maybe you can find some baking bananas at the market in Omaha, Mom, and try this out. It's wild!

With love, Bill

Ed Kenney

E d Kenney is the closest thing to a "rock star chef" in Hawaii. He's got the tattoos. The rabid following. And some swagger, to boot.

But Kenney didn't always have his sights set on a life in the culinary world. He earned a business degree in Colorado and delved headlong into commercial real estate on Oahu. After pounding the pavement and pushing papers for four years, he packed the smallest pack he could find and set out on the road. He toured the globe, eagerly and anxiously awaiting his next meal at every stop. He claims it was over a bowl of pho on a street corner in Hanoi, Vietnam, where his "transformation" began. As different as the people he met at each stop were, all were bonded over warm meals. Through the flavors of any region, you could understand, appreciate and relish in the culture in which you stood.

Ed made it his mission to share with visitors and residents in Hawaii what his experience on the islands has meant. He still plates every dish today with this in mind.

His restaurant Town has earned multiple local awards; he opened Downtown in the Hawaii State Art Museum (HiSAM; it closed a few years ago) and Uptown Events in 2009 where he caters private functions. More recently, Kaimuki Superette and Mud Hen Water established Kenney as the "King of Kaimuki" eateries, each within eyeshot of one another off Waialae and 9th Avenues.

Ed Kenney is a proponent of food and sustainability education for the youth of Hawaii, which has teamed him up with Jack and Kim Johnson's Kokua Foundation, as well as Sustain Hawaii. He sits on the board of Ma'o Organic Farms and guest teaches or speaks at the Culinary Institute of the Pacific.

Roasted Mai'a Maoli (Native Heirloom Banana) with Curry Butter and Bacon

THERE ARE A LOT of things to love about what chef and restaurateur Ed Kenney has done to evolve the Honolulu dining scene during the last decade. One of those includes his fun style of preparing common dishes with a bit of a twist—much of the time reminding us of simpler days—like when we were children.

This baked banana is reminiscent of a baked potato, in both presentation and that you get to "dress it up" however you like with the sides Kenney suggests you serve with the dish. This is a fun recipe to try midweek to liven up the family dinner table.

Preheat the oven to 350°F and roast the bananas in a baking dish for 30 minutes. (Any plump cooking banana will suffice.)

Meanwhile, prepare the curry butter by combining the softened and salted butter, Madras curry powder, allspice and crushed red pepper flakes.

Next, prepare the condiments that you'll serve alongside the baked bananas: green onion, eggs, bacon strips, toasted coconut and roasted peanuts in separate finger bowls.

Remove the bananas from the oven (they should be black) and place them on individual plates. Cut a slit down the top-facing side (like you would a baked potato) and squeeze to open the pocket. Top each banana with a few tablespoons of the curry butter and your choice of condiments to taste.

This dish is particularly delicious when accompanied by an off-dry Riesling, an Alsatian Gewürztraminer or an India Pale Ale beer.

Serves 4

4 yellow, ripe baking bananas

4 ounces salted butter, softened

2 teaspoons Madras curry powder

¼ teaspoon allspice, ground

¼ teaspoon crushed red pepper flakes

Condiments

¼ cup green onion, thinly sliced, green parts only

2 hard-boiled eggs, chopped

8 bacon strips, crispy and chopped

¼ cup toasted coconut

¼ cup roasted peanuts, chopped

Dear Mom,

There's a girl in my son Luke's class whose father is Roy Yamaguchi—quite possibly the biggest culinary success story to ever come out of Hawaii. (More on this later.) As a restaurateur myself, it's fun to know I have someone to chat with at the kids' social and school events. Yet the "small world nature" of life in the islands very nearly rained on our parade a few years ago. Let me explain.

When I hired our executive chef, Ronnie Nasuti, he was formerly running Roy's kitchen in Hawaii Kai. You would probably remember the restaurant, it's the first "fancy" place

that I took you when you came to visit, after I'd had some success and was excited to take you out to dinner. If it still isn't striking a bell . . . you loved it. Remember the story I told you about the first time I ate there? I ordered ahi tuna and asked for it to be cooked through, and the waiter suggested I try seared raw. My mind was blown in six directions and forever altered the course of my eating in Hawaii.

A business owner hiring away a top talent isn't a unique occurrence. But here in the islands it's not long until you're destined to bump into someone you're not entirely prepared to come face-to-face with.

Three months after I'd hired Ronnie, we were invited to an event called Taste of the Hawaiian Range, held in a ballroom at the prestigious Halekulani hotel. The culinary dine-around featured fifteen of Hawaii's top chefs statewide, each plating a dish that spotlighted locally ranched meat. Ronnie and his wife joined Tracy and I.

As soon as we opened the doors, directly in front of me was Roy. Before any of us had a chance to adjust, Roy Yamaguchi was standing right in front of all four of us with no one else around him . . . and no escape for any of us!

Without so much as blinking, Roy extended a hand to me and shook mine firmly. "Glad you made it. It's nice to see you," he said. With that, the tension was diffused. He's a consummate business man, and his experience and maturity really shined here. At first, I was unsure if he really put it together—who I was and what I'd done—as he reached out so quickly and with such sincere friendliness.

After a few cocktails to settle the nerves for all of us, it ended up being a fantastic night of sampling amazing meats and great drinks. There was a live band playing to really up the classiness of the event. The four of us ended up seated around a small cocktail table outside on the lanai, sipping coffee and sampling desserts. The moon was bright, we could hear the lapping of the waves just beyond the hotel. Another magical night in paradise.

A few weeks later, Ronnie was just starting to integrate his methodology and practices into the Tiki's kitchen. Things were beginning to gel. We all attended a local magazine food awards reception where accolades were handed out to restaurants and chefs for service the calendar year prior. In the last and biggest award of the night, Roy's Hawaii Kai—where I hired Ronnie away from—won "Best Restaurant." The president of Roy Yamaguchi's restaurant empire, Rainer Kumbroch, accepted the award, said a few words, and walked off the stage with a giant magnum of champagne. He walked directly over to our table and placed it gracefully in front of chef Ronnie, without saying a word, then walked off.

Ronnie's wife started crying. I thought we were going to lose our new chef before we even had a chance to print his name in our menu. I couldn't see this as anything but a very classy act by the Roy's team, and confirmation of what I experienced at the Halekulani weeks prior when Roy shook my hand. To recognize the work Ronnie did as executive chef out in Hawaii Kai for ten years, and then send him off with that tribute . . . I have nothing but respect for that Roy's team. Same goes to Ronnie for standing proud that day, and even prouder for the day he took the reigns inside the kitchen at Tiki's Grill & Bar.

With love, Bill

Roy Yamaguchi

Roy Yamaguchi is Hawaii's most recognizable chef and restaurateur. There isn't a culinary career person who doesn't admire—and aspire—to emulate the successes Roy has achieved. And his story is emblematic of just how far hard work, drive and passion for greatness can take you.

Born in Tokyo, Japan, to a Hawaii-born father and an Okinawan mother, Yamaguchi spent his formative years in the bustling Japanese metropolis while visiting his grandfather on Maui, who owned a small restaurant in Wailuku. His immediate taking to the mash-up of island flavors with a backdrop of Japanese influence were enough to push the ambitious youth to apply and graduate from the Culinary Institute of America (CIA) in Hyde Park, New York—at the ripe ol' age of nineteen. He worked his way through storied kitchens in California before opening his own restaurant, which he endured for four years.

He packed up and headed for Hawaii in 1988, digging in with furious intention to open his first signature Roy's. Here's where the magic began: Roy proceeded to turn the islands' culinary scene on its proverbial head. Where tourists were being fed macadamia nut crusted fish (often overcooked, almost always frozen, and rarely from Hawaiian waters), Yamaguchi started plating fresh local catch with delicate European-style sauces. The combination opened the hearts and palates of island residents statewide, who clamored to his upscale eatery in Hawaii Kai for special occasions. This earned Yamaguchi not only a devout following for life, but a small army of young chefs, hospitality business folk and, heck, even dishwashers who wanted "in" on whatever he was cooking. Onward Roy Yamaguchi pressed, opening thirty more restaurants in Japan and China as well as across the United States, from California and Arizona to Texas and Florida.

Yamaguchi went on to publish multiple books, earned a James Beard award, hosted his own long-running television show, competed on *Top Chef Masters* and *Iron Chef America*, cofounded the Hawaii Food & Wine Festival (with Alan Wong) and sits on multiple boards that champion the culinary arts in Hawaii as well as nationally. He's given commencement speeches at his alma mater (CIA) and led the culinary aspect of Brand USA—a government supported travel and tourism vehicle that markets travel to the United States in dozens of countries around the globe.

As one of the twelve founders of Hawaii Regional Cuisine, he has employed a legion of now successful chefs and restaurateurs, including Tiki's Grill & Bar executive chef, Ronnie Nasuti, who ran Roy's original outpost in Hawaii Kai for more than a decade.

Bubu-Crusted Hawaiian Mahimahi with Fresh Tomato Sambal

IT'S NO SECRET that Roy was the first Hawaii-based chef to receive worldwide recognition for his style of preparing uniquely Hawaiian ingredients. Here, he makes use of various types of lettuces and fruits for a base salad, then ups the ante by coating the fish with a tangy tomato sambal and crusting with sweet rice crackers. It's Hawaii meets India by way of Thailand and back to Hawaii again. Yet, you can produce this in your own kitchen, anywhere across the globe.

Crust
In a medium bowl, mix all ingredients together.

Fresh Tomato Sambal
In a separate bowl, combine all the ingredients; add the tomatoes last—when you add them, squeeze them slightly to release some of their juices into the sauce.

Fish
Season the mahimahi with salt and pepper all over, then press one side of the fish into the bubu crust so that the mixture sticks to the fish. Put the crusted side face down into a hot frying pan coated with a little olive oil and cook until golden brown. Flip the fish and cook till desired doneness.

Salad
We utilize a variety of local lettuces, and you can, too, by visiting your local farmers' market or store that features fresh greens.

Serves 4

Crust
¼ cup chicken flour

½ cup panko

2 tablespoons bubu arare

1½ tablespoons Madras curry

2 tablespoons furikake

Salt and pepper to taste

Fresh Tomato Sambal
2 shallots, sliced thin

2 tablespoons cilantro, chopped

1 tablespoon garlic, chopped

1 Hawaiian chili pepper, minced

1 cup rice wine vinegar

1 cup shoyu

2 tablespoons brown sugar

2 tablespoons fish sauce

Juice of 1 lemon

Salt and black pepper to taste

1 pint Ho Farm Fiesta tomatoes, halved

Fish
4 (6-ounce) pieces of local mahimahi

Olive oil for cooking

Salt and pepper

Salad
Kula butter lettuce

Kula romaine

North Shore red leaf lettuce

Frisée

Radish

Sprouts

Hearts of palm, shaved

Mango

Green papaya

Cherry tomatoes

Dear Mom,

I first tasted the creations of Isaac Bancaco when he replaced a longtime chef at Pineapple Grill on the grounds of the stunning, pine tree-lined Kapalua Resort. He stepped into a role that came with a predetermined following, and he took the reins gracefully. Adding more local ingredients and a subtle Maui flair to dishes, Isaac won me over with succulent braised short ribs and a half dozen other dishes that found their way to our table one evening.

There's a lot to love about Isaac as a chef who epitomizes Hawaii's new cuisine: his dedication to sourcing local ingredients, his Maui upbringing on the slopes of Haleakala with a family of watermen and cowboys, the varied culinary influences of his multicultural heritage (Chinese, Japanese, Hawaiian, Filipino). Yet there's another aspect to his personality that really shines for me.

In the spring of 2014, I attended a special dinner on Maui's lush North Shore, just outside of Hana. This area, Mom, is incredibly special, what a lot of people would call "old Hawaii." Rainforests, waterfalls every which way, rich cultural sites, botanical gardens and not a lot of people. (Jim Nabors owns a macadamia nut farm here!) I'd been invited to support a local, independent film called *I am Haloa* about a trio of high school kids who opted to sustain themselves solely on *kalo*, or taro root, and how it connected them with the roots of their Hawaiian ancestors. The benefit was an alfresco dinner in the picturesque Kahanu Botanical Gardens. Among the chefs prepping the meal—which was served at a long, creekside table that sat sixty—were Lee Anne Wong and Isaac Bancaco.

We spent the early part of the afternoon exploring *heiau* (stone temples of great significance to ancient Hawaiians), learning about sugar cane, walking through the biggest collection of banana plant varietals in the hemisphere, all the while snacking on taro canapes.

When we headed back to the table for dinner, Isaac walked from seat to seat, conversing with everyone about what brought them to the dinner and what they liked about the dishes

he and Wong were serving. Although the dinner wasn't for his benefit, he was a gracious host, making sure everyone had a chance to meet the young filmmakers we were there to support. He explained the significance of what we were eating, how taro was worthy of playing the lead role in the film. And he shared some stories about the significance of eating taro during his youth, and how it connected him (today) as a chef to his ancestors.

Since that event, I've followed chef Isaac on social media and seen how he lives the spirit of aloha. Whether freediving and spearfishing with friends or paddling into a double overhead wave, he's got the same smile on his face and a warmth about him. In this day and age, when a lot of local people—not just in Hawaii, but everywhere—have their guard up, Isaac seems to want to share his knowledge about Hawaii and its foods with everyone. Those of us who get to sample the culinary wonders he plates are the better for it. We're the lucky ones.

With love, Bill

Isaac Bancaco

Whan I think about culinary stars who've come full circle, Maui born-and-raised chef Isaac Bancaco comes to mind first. Raised on the sun-drenched, red clay slopes of Haleakala, he left the islands for his first "big show" cooking gig at Ming Tsai's Blue Ginger restaurant outside of Boston. He worked seamlessly alongside Tsai on *Iron Chef America*, helping him to deliver Bobby Flay his first loss on national television. Isaac then headed west for a stint in Roy Yamaguchi's California outpost, hoping to scratch an itch for the taste of home. A bit of stardom in his eyes, Isaac returned to Maui to elevate the kitchens of Pineapple Grill at Kapalua and Humuhumunukunukuapua'a at the Grand Wailea Resort, where he earned multiple accolades.

When the developers of Hyatt's über-hip boutique property, Andaz Wailea, were looking for someone to spearhead an ambitious dining concept and anchor the hotel's swank, international jet-set vibe, albeit with some connections to the Hawaii food experience, Isaac was the clear choice. At Ka'ana Kitchen, the open format, multiple chef's tables and unique menu were a blank slate on which Isaac could paint a culinary masterpiece—and boy, has he done just that.

Considering the volume of food it takes to feed guests at a tony Wailea resort property, it's a feat that Isaac uses up to 85 percent local produce and proteins at Ka'ana Kitchen. Yet chat with him for a few minutes, and it's not hard to see the means to his end. He's passionate about using produce from local farms in Kula, Makawao and Haiku, where he grew up. He's a champion of the smallest farmers, working to support a community whose sole aim is to take advantage of Hawaii's gentle climate and fertile soil to put forth the best product. In a single year, Isaac might use product from up to twenty different Maui farmers. It's the best kind of win-win: Supporting the sustainable farming community on this small island while giving visitors to his restaurant the opportunity to taste the amazing flavors of Maui.

Most recently, a chance encounter opened the door for Isaac to plant dozens of chili pepper plants on the hotel grounds for crafting his own brand of hot sauce—just one example of the lengths he'll go to "bump up" the offerings he plates. Wherever Isaac goes, I will follow . . . with an eager palate.

Hanger Steak with Green Papaya Salad

ONE OF the most striking things about this dish—besides Chef Isaac's presentation, each in it's own cast iron pan in order to retain heat while you devour this steak—is the balance of flavors in the accompaniment. The punch of the kimchi and other zesty steak marinade is paralleled by the green papaya salad with Thai vinaigrette. By just perfectly searing your hanger steak, you'll win over a loyal following to any and all dinner parties you throw.

Add all the ingredients together and mix well. Pour the marinade over the hanger steaks, making sure to cover completely. Marinate for a minimum of 24 hours. Finish on grill over medium-high heat

Peel the green papaya, cut in half and remove the seeds, then slice thinly with a knife or use a mandolin and cut julienne style. Remove the seeds from the bell pepper and slice thinly. Peel the outer skin of the onion and slice thinly. Then place all ingredients in a bowl. Mince all the herbs and add to the bowl.

In small bowl, whisk the vinaigrette ingredients together and toss into the green papaya salad. Finish by adding salt and pepper to taste.

Serves 4

Hanger Steak Marinade

2 cups sugar

2 cups tamari

½ cup ginger, minced

½ cup garlic, minced

¼ cup green onion, sliced

½ cup kimchi base

¼ cup toasted sesame seeds

2 limes, zest and juice

½ cup water

4 (3½-ounce) hanger steaks

Papaya Salad

1 each green papaya and red bell pepper

½ onion

2 tablespoons cilantro

2 tablespoons mint

2 tablespoons basil

Salt and pepper to taste

Thai Vinaigrette

½ cup lime juice

¼ cup fish sauce

¼ cup white sugar

1 tablespoon red bell pepper, diced small

1 tablespoon jalapeños, diced small

1 tablespoon shallots, diced small

1 tablespoon celery, diced small

Dear Mom,

As I've been writing to you, the process of composing these letters has led me to realize a few things. I find it pretty amazing that merely taking a few minutes to sit and write to you puts things about my world here in Hawaii into fresh perspective. This story really highlights what I'm talking about.

For the past few years, Tracy and I have been lucky to call Kevin Hanney a friend. We met him around the time he was opening his restaurant, 12th Ave Grill in Kaimuki. His son Collin is the same age as our Max. Now they are in the same class together.

Have you ever noticed that when a lot of famous chefs get asked what they cook at home, they say, "I don't cook at home" or "I eat cereal" or something similar? It's understandable: They put it all out there on the job, and the last thing they want to do at home is prep, cook and clean more food. But I can't help but think: What a bum deal for their families!

Kevin is the polar opposite. When he invited us to our first barbecue at his home, he prefaced it with, "It will be very casual. Come in shorts, slippers and T-shirts." So we grabbed a bottle of wine, put on our slippers (what we'd call "flip-flops" back home), bought some chips and arrived as requested.

On the counter in his kitchen was a spread the likes of which I haven't seen in Hawaii, ever. A dozen cured meats. Pickled vegetables. Mustards and sauces. Toast points. Garnishes of all sorts. It felt more like the appetizer hour at a wedding. And there was Kevin, in shorts and barefoot, like it was any typical Sunday.

He cooked as we talked, casually barbecuing skirts steaks that he topped with an amazing kimchi—the Korean fermented cabbage that has a cultish following here in Hawaii. I remember heaping forkful after forkful of the glistening red kimchi on my plate, making sure I had a good amount to accompany each bite of Kevin's perfectly cooked steak. (If anyone would have told me twenty years ago I'd be feasting on fermented cabbage, I'd have laughed.)

Kevin also served up a thick pork chop. He plated it for us with a potato pancake and a baked spiced apple, served halved and seeded. Growing up when I did, all I could think of was the "pork chops and apple sauce" episode of *The Brady Bunch*. But after one bite, I wasn't thinking about anything except what was happening in my mouth—a perfect fusion of flavor.

I looked at Tracy, and she was doing the same! Inside the house, the kids were particularly quiet—always a worrisome sign. But when I peeked in, they were all shoveling Kevin's charcuterie into their mouths, barely breathing between bites. It was an unexpected feast unlike any I'd experienced at a "casual" Sunday afternoon barbecue. And I'm happy to say

I've been blessed to experience it many times since.

When people ask me what Kevin's restaurant is like, I find that I can't aptly describe it. I might call it "New Age American Bistro" one day, "American-Hawaiian regional" the next and a combination of the two on yet a third occasion. But after considering the way in which Kevin approaches food—both at home and at his establishments—I realized something: This is a fresh approach to dining in America, one that incorporates and reflects our multicultural communities. Not just in Hawaii but everywhere these days, it seems there are people from all sorts of backgrounds and ethnicities living in close quarters. Inevitably, the food is the first place where the mingling happens, and it's usually well received.

The chalkboard menu, the bistro bar seating, the banquettes against the walls—12th Ave Grill feels like an American bistro. But scan the menu, and you find hints of Chinese, Japanese, Filipino, Korean, Thai—all sorts of cultures represented alongside things like cured meats, a devoutly European or American standby.

Maybe it's because I've gotten to know Kevin and his family, but none of this comes across gimmicky or gratuitous at 12th Ave Grill. Everything has its place on the menu; the flavors work well together, the dishes complement each other. I've really come to appreciate this approach. Not every diner can put a finger on what makes the experience there so special, but I think it's quite simply Kevin's love for food of all types and his painstaking efforts to figure out the best ways to merge them. That and the fact that he doesn't turn it off when he's at home but instead cooks and shares with family and friends. Well, that just shows it's a part of who he is as a culinarian. Of course we're the luckier for it!

With love, Bill

Kevin Hanney

Kevin Hanney is the owner of 12th Ave Grill and part owner of Koko Head Cafe (with Lee Anne Wong). He's been immersed in the restaurant industry his entire adult life. From working front-of-house in his early teens, he moved behind the stoves at an organic farm in the Finger Lakes region of New York in 1978, finding early inspiration in what he could achieve with the yield from a single acre.

Kevin moved to California in the early 1980s to study solar architecture and renewable energy, all the while working as a chef during the heyday of California Cuisine. He launched a catering business in Santa Cruz, where he earned a reputation as a chef that prepared seasonal menus with local offerings—novel at the time.

A decade later Hawaii called; he was asked to attend and cook at a food and wine festival at the Mauna Kea Resort on Hawaii Island. He saw a new opportunity to work with local farmers, fishermen and purveyors and in 2004 opened 12th Ave Grill, an American brasserie-style restaurant with a local, sustainable philosophy. Whether he's sourcing grass-fed beef or pork from Amy's Pig Farm (Shinsato), using Niihau lamb or exploring other whole-animal practices, Kevin is consistently employing sustainable practices.

Although he doesn't receive as much fanfare as other island chefs, Kevin's 12th Ave Grill has earned multiple magazine and people's choice awards. He was instrumental in bringing Lee Anne Wong to Honolulu, partnering with her at Koko Head Cafe—the original location of 12th Ave Grill prior to its move a block away in the Honolulu neighborhood of Kaimuki. Both restaurants continue to thrill guests with unique platings of American fare with a Hawaii spin and an eye on sustainable practices.

LAMB

Coconut Porter Braised Lamb Shanks with Sweet Potato and Corn Hash

CHEF HANNEY offers this rich and hearty dish that makes great use of a local Hawaii-based beer. You can add any porter beer you can find at your local market. [Hint: Try experimenting with those infused with coffee, chocolate or other rich fruits.] The results here—tender, peel-with-a-fork lamb—melds perfectly with Kevin's sweet potato and corn hash. Dig in!

Porter Braised Niihau Lamb Shanks
Season the lamb shanks liberally with salt and pepper. If your stock contains salt in it, reduce the amount of salt. In a heavy bottom pan on medium-high heat, add the oil. Once the oil is hot enough (when a drop of water sizzles), add the lamb shanks. Brown on all sides, approximately 3 to 4 minutes per side. Remove the shanks and discard the oil. Place the pan back on the stove and put the shanks back in and add the remaining ingredients. Bring to a simmer and reduce the heat to low. Cover for 3 to 4 hours until meat is tender. (Alternatively, cook in a 325°F oven.) Allow the shanks to rest in the liquid for at least 30 minutes with the heat off.

Remove the shanks and strain the liquid into another pot and reduce the liquid by half. Remove any fat from the top of the sauce. Serve as a sauce with shanks.

For best results, chill the lamb in liquid overnight; this will allow for a juicer shank and make it easier to remove the fat. Just reheat in the oven on medium heat until hot.

Molokai Sweet Potato Corn Hash
In a sauté pan over medium-high heat add the oil. Add the diced sweet potatoes and sauté them until they start to brown. Add all the remaining ingredients except parsley, salt and pepper. Continue to sauté until the potatoes begin to soften and brown. Season with salt and pepper and finish with the parsley. For a slightly richer version, finish with the unsalted butter.

Sautéed Ho Farms Rainbow Swiss Chard
Rough chop the Swiss chard. Over medium-high heat add the garlic and oil until the garlic begins to brown. This will happen fast—so have all ingredients ready to add. Add the Swiss chard and toss immediately. Cook until the chard begins to wilt and season with salt and pepper. Remove from the heat and serve. Swiss chard will continue to cook from its own heat.

To serve, place 6 tablespoons of the Molokai sweet potato hash in the bottom left corner of a square bowl. Place the sautéed Swiss chard in bottom right corner of the bowl, then place the hot lamb shanks between the hash and the chard. Pour ¼ cup of braising jus over the lamb shank.

Serves 4 to 6

Lamb Shanks
4 (6–20 ounce) lamb shanks
Salt and pepper
1 cup light olive oil or vegetable oil
2 (12-ounce) cans of Maui Brewing Co. Coconut porter
1 tablespoon grainy Dijon mustard
4 gloves of garlic, crushed
1 small onion, chopped
4 sprigs of fresh thyme (or 1 teaspoon dry)
2–3 bay leafs
4 cups veal or beef stock, or enough to cover

Molokai Sweet Potato Corn Hash
1 tablespoon light olive oil or vegetable oil
1 pound diced and peeled Molokai sweet potatoes (or Okinawan sweet potatoes)
½ cup diced red bell peppers
½ cup diced yellow bell peppers
½ cup diced onion
1 cup Kahuku corn removed from the cob
1 teaspoon chopped garlic
½ teaspoon chopped parsley
Salt and pepper to taste
1 teaspoon unsalted butter, optional

Sautéed Ho Farms Rainbow Swiss Chard
1 pound Swiss chard, cleaned and washed
½ teaspoon chopped garlic
1 tablespoon olive oil
Salt and pepper to taste

Epilogue

When Bill Tobin approached me with the concept for this book, I had already interviewed many, many chefs. I'd eaten dishes from culinary talent around the globe, some of which were made specially for me. I'd nibbled entrées crafted by chef-artisans who had full knowledge they would appear in the shiny magazine stories that likely found their way onto your kitchen counters and coffee tables. And I had dined incognito inside legendary dining rooms (as well as hole-in-the-wall gems), only later to meet and interview the chef(s), grilling them on technique and execution.

I'd slurped fresh mussels, grilled sardines and twirled homemade pasta onto a fork in Amalfi, Italy—in an Etruscan cave, no less. There was the inhaling of rosti with red cabbage and perfectly grilled venison at a grotto high in the mountain climes of Switzerland. I've languished at the luxury of unpasteurized (and prized) cheese in southern France, where the best accompaniment was the warm Mediterranean breeze. And of course, I've traipsed all over the cooking front lines (with chefs of all ilk) in the proving grounds of Manhattan, New York, from where I hail.

I share this with you, reader, not as some badge of honor. Nor to rub in your face how many delightful (and paid for by someone else) meals I've consumed. I do so merely to lead you to the "why" I decided to live such a life. It's simple, really. Because of the stories.

The chef has always been one of the more unique species throughout humanity. People who spend most waking moments of their lives pondering flavor profiles solely for you and I to enjoy. They endure a lifetime of honing a craft that blends science with technique and opinion; in hopes that you'll heap forkfuls of whatever they make into your mouth with enough gusto to stand up, leave their establishments, and tell all your friends and family how amazing the such-and-such you just ate was.

If you were to read the actual job description of a chef, you—as a sane human being—would never consider the life it entails. Up at the crack of dawn to receive product, wrangling a staff of misfits (many of whom you'll need multiple linguistic skills to communicate with), hours of menu development, honing final dishes, overseeing a front-of-house staff that won't blow your hard work through crappy service and then all the joys of after hours—including cleanup, accounting and plans for the following day. That's . . . all in a single day. Only to be revisited for the next six days in a row. Not for the faint of heart.

And yet, heart is the reason most chefs tie on an apron and sharpen their knives every morning. They sink a combination of their bravado, skills, ingenuity and provenance into a meal for you. Just . . . for you. To nourish your body. In hopes that a steady stream of happy regulars ensures they can afford to keep the lights on. Or pay a mortgage and put a kid or two through school.

Like most writers, I have a bit of a wandering attention span. At the onset of my writing career, I resided in New York City—arguably the capital of the written word, as well as a melting pot of cultures and their respective cuisines.

On one occasion, I found myself in Honolulu on a press trip, circa 1998. On the way over, I read up on traditional Hawaiian foods, the Hawaii Regional Cuisine movement, and who the "it" chefs across the islands were at that moment. There didn't seem to be a cohesive "movement" at the time; it was as if people were just so damn thrilled to be in Hawaii, and, "Hey! There's some decent food here too!" was enough. (This was all about to change, dramatically.)

However, even at this lull, my intrigue was piqued nearly every time we sat down for a meal. First, the manner in which present-day Hawaiian chefs were interpreting the cuisine of their ancestors, ever-so-slightly different from one eatery to the next. There were the subtle nuances that came from other Polynesian island nations—Samoa, Tahiti, Fiji and so on. Then, the injection of plantation-era cultures who took up residence across the isles during the agricultural boom of the late 1800s, which included Chinese, Japanese, Filipino, Thai, Vietnamese. Then, there were the chefs from far-flung locales like France, Finland, London, Chicago—you name it—who were "bitten" by the aloha bug and reimagined themselves as chefs telling their version of the foods of the Pacific, factoring in their respective backgrounds, schooling and experience.

Meld in how much each restaurant I visited that trip needed to depend on visitors' palates (vs. locals'), and you had a mash-up of so many presentations of the same dishes, it was dizzying . . . in the most wonderfully spectacular way.

Continued

The allure of nearly every dish I sampled in those few days, within a small geographic proximity (not far beyond Waikiki), whet my appetite but did not sate my hunger—the door had been opened, and I wanted back in.

Cut to four years later and, in the midst of a particularly icy New York City winter, those flavors still whirled inside my head. I packed up my Upper West Side apartment, stuffed what I could into a pair of duffel bags, boxed up my bicycle and placed my 1974 Ford Bronco (stored safely in upstate New York) onto a westbound train and then on a Matson vessel sailing for the islands.

I understand the allure—the call—for the flavors of Hawaii. I quickly met families who would overnight limu ahi poke (packed in dry ice) to their kids at mainland colleges—more in hopes that they would stay in school rather than return home early just for "a taste." I endured a number of *pau hana* barbecue or potluck dinners where guests would debate the best Hawaiian chili water recipe to the point of wrestling. And maybe you, too, have been privy to the spectacle that is an Oahu resident buying an extra Hawaiian Airlines seat to stack up boxes of fresh Krispy Kreme doughnuts in order to be the family hero, or help kids with their school bake sale. (Thank goodness those inter-island flights are only twenty minutes; the scent of fresh doughnuts fills a plane quickly and deeply.)

So when Bill Tobin came to me, he began by saying he could sense the familiarity with which I wrote about Hawaii's food. Although an outsider to this beautiful place, he understood how it entrapped me, embraced me, and appreciated how I was able to tell the stories of the chefs, dishes, farms and ingredients across the islands. And . . . that he had a story of his own he was itching to share.

As you've hopefully garnered from the pages of this book, Bill's passion for Hawaii forever altered the course of his life. A self-proclaimed farm boy from Tekamah, Nebraska, his idea of "breaking out" of the norm was a stint in the National Guard, schooling in the Pacific, and a business degree that would bring him home, eventually, to the Midwest. But along the way, a fellow

bouncer, bartender, girlfriend (or two) and mentor would reveal to him a unique Hawaiian flavor. Then another. And another.

At some point, there was no turning back for Bill. He opened Tiki's Grill & Bar, and the rest, as they say, is history. A wife and three boys, who now attend a prestigious school on the same small island that the current president of the United States of America was raised on, doesn't fall short on Bill. He appreciates even the littlest of things, and has a genuine nature that dovetails with the aloha spirit.

Bill's desire to share these personal letters to his mom, who has now passed, is sincere. Not just in his passion for the food and flavors of Hawaii, but in his journey in discovering them. In appreciating their uniqueness. And fully knowing that every single day of the year, someone steps off a plane onto a Hawaiian island for the first time, eyes a plate of fresh poke, a crispy fried banana lumpia or unwraps a steaming pork lau lau—brings a forkful to the mouth—and is hooked for life.

I hope you enjoy the stories—and the flavors that make them flourish—inside these pages. Try and challenge yourself to prepare a few of the recipes our featured chefs carefully selected to share, in hopes that you can impart some of their aloha onto your dinner guests. May you fall in love with these islands again and again, bite after bite.

Mahalo, Brian Berusch

Feel free to share photos and stories of your recipes at TikisGrill.com/FoodToWriteHomeAbout. We'll be sharing updates, new recipes and events there as well.

Colophon

Cameron + Company
6 Petaluma Blvd. North, Suite B-6
Petaluma, CA 94952
www.cameronbooks.com

Publisher: *Chris Gruener*
Creative Director: *Iain R. Morris*
Designer: *Suzi Hutsell*
Editor: *Brian Berusch*
Proofreaders: *Jan Hughes, Cristal Cardenas Sanchez*

All photographs copyright © 2016 Olivier Koning unless noted below.

Photographs courtesy of Bill Tobin: 7, 10, 11, 18, 24, 32 (inset), 40, 41, 48 (inset), 56, 64 (inset), 72, 73, 80, 81, 88, 95 (inset), 102, 103, 110 (inset), 118 (inset), 126, 127, 134, 142 (inset), 150, 158, 167 (inset)

Photographs courtesy of Shutterstock: 19, 32, 34, 38, 48, 57, 60, 62, 64, 78, 89, 94, 96, 110, 116, 117, 118, 132, 135, 142, 151, 159, 160, 164, 166, 172

Illustrations courtesy of Shutterstock

ISBN: 978-1-937359-87-4

Manufactured in China

10 9 8 7 6 5 4 3 2 1

CAMERON + COMPANY would like to thank Bill Tobin for allowing us the honor of publishing this extremely personal and important book that showcases Hawaii's current food scene so beautifully; Brian Berusch for introducing us to Bill and for his overall editorial direction; Suzi Hutsell for capturing the Hawaiian sensibilities so perfectly with the book's design; Iain Morris for his inspiring creative direction; Jan Hughes for her copy editing and proofreading; and Cristal Cardenas Sanchez for her additional proofreading.